The Bargaining Bride

How to Have
the Wedding
of Your Dreams
without Paying
the Bills
of Your
Nightmares

Shirit Kronzon, Ph.D., & Andrew Ward, Ph.D.

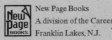

New Page Books
A division of the Career Press
Franklin Lakes, N.J.

THE BARGAINING BRIDE

EDITED AND TYPESET BY KATE HENCHES

Cover design by Lu Rossman/Digi Dog Design

Illustrations by Stephanie Ward

Printed in the U.S.A. by Book-mart Press

To order this title, please call toll-free 1-800-CAREER-1 (NJ and Canada: 201-848-0310) to order using VISA or MasterCard, or for further information on books from Career Press.

The Career Press, Inc., 3 Tice Road, PO Box 687,
Franklin Lakes, NJ 07417
www.careerpress.com
www.newpagebooks.com

Library of Congress Cataloging-in-Publication Data

Available upon request.

Dedication

To my husband.

–S.K.

To my parents.

–A.W.

Acknowledgments

From the moment that Shirit first conceived of the idea for this book, we have been assisted and supported by a host of family, colleagues, and friends. We would especially like to acknowledge the contribution of Barry Schwartz, who read several drafts and provided wise counsel on many occasions. We would also like to thank Mark Lepper and Tom Gilovich, who helped us locate representation, ably embodied by our wonderful agent Stacey Glick. Michael Ward furnished valuable legal assistance (it sure helps to have a lawyer in the family!), as did Mark Huppin. We are indebted as well to Diane Schaffer and Rosalie Feeney, who freely shared their wedding expertise with us, and to the many individuals who provided us with stories of wedding triumphs and challenges. Thanks also go to the Wharton School of Business and Swarthmore College, and we are of course grateful to the capable team at Career Press. In addition, we acknowledge the love and support of our respective families: The Kronzons, the Anoliks, and the Wards.

Despite her busy schedule as director of several children's programs, Stephanie Ward found time to provide the wonderful illustrations included in this book (it sure helps to have an artist in the family!), for which we are eternally grateful.

Finally, Shirit would like to express her most heartfelt gratitude to the love of her life, her husband Adam Anolik, who offered unwavering support throughout this project. Without Adam, there would have been no wedding and, thus, no *Bargaining Bride*.

—Shirit Kronzon and Andrew Ward

Contents

Introduction

Congratulations! You're engaged! You have found your match: the man you love, the man of your dreams. Now you must plan your wedding. All you have to do is (1) purchase a wedding gown and pick dresses for the bridesmaids; (2) design the ceremony; (3) reserve a reception hall; (4) hire a caterer; (5) order a cake; (6) book musicians; (7) select a florist; (8) choose a photographer and videographer; (9) buy invitations; (10) accommodate all your in-laws' requests; and (11) wonder if your mother would ever speak to you again if you eloped instead. Okay, you get the point: If you are like most brides, you will soon be spending the next several months preparing for the most important day of your life. There will be lots of details to consider, lots of decisions to make, and lots of negotiations in which to participate.

So where do you begin? For each part of the wedding that you intend to plan, you can count on meeting with any number of potential service providers. You might visit 10 reception halls, five photographers, and several florists. You might check out half a dozen bridal boutiques and a dozen caterers, or vice-versa. You might listen to several bands, orchestras, and DJs—and that's not counting your cousin's garage band, which he swears knows how to play "O Promise Me" on the electric guitar.

And then, after meeting with all those individuals, you'll want to settle on the best provider for each service. You'll want that provider to give you the best service for the lowest possible price. Indeed, as you've no doubt surmised by now, at the core of planning a wedding is a skill that you might not have realized that you need: You have to know how to negotiate. The notion that negotiation is involved in planning your wedding might be a bit daunting. After all, many people would prefer root-canal surgery to bargaining with someone—and that reluctance to negotiate may apply especially to us women, according to Linda Babcock and Sara Laschever, authors of *Women Don't Ask: Negotiation and the Gender Divide*. But fear not—I am here to help.

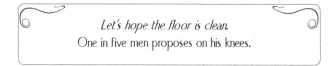

Let's hope the floor is clean.
One in five men proposes on his knees.

Weddings Are Expensive

For many people, a wedding is second only to buying a house in terms of how much money they spend. But generally we tend to get married first, and buy a house second. By the time we get to the house, we know we have to negotiate; after all, there is a lot of money at stake. But consider, when it comes to weddings, you could easily spend the following: $1500 for a dress, $4000 for rings, and $1000 for music. If you want your guests to eat something, you're talking anywhere between $20 to $60 per person for a cocktail buffet, to as much as $100 or more for a full sit-down dinner. Stationery for 100 simple invitations is likely to set you back between $175 and $200, but if, like many people, you feel this is one time when folks actually need an engraved invitation (and you thought that was just an expression), $600 may be a better estimate. Indeed, with flowers, photography, cake, and catering included, experts estimate that the average wedding cost is more than $20,000 (see Table 1 on page 18 for a breakdown of typical wedding expenses). This number may be much higher in large metropolitan areas such as Los Angeles or New York City—and let's not even talk about Hawaii. Of course, these estimates are just averages: Go into any store and you will find that prices can be much higher for the particulars that you have in mind.

Weddings Are a Business

Yes, it's important to try to save money when planning a wedding. But not by settling for less. Instead, we negotiate for more. After all, a wedding is a business arrangement. We don't think of it as negotiation, but it is, and it involves a lot of money. We may like to think of the various vendors as nice people who want to help us plan the wedding. Maybe we've had an image of little old ladies who help squeeze us into our gowns. These ladies want us to fit into gowns, all right, just as long as they're the ones selling us the gowns. In fact, maybe you've noticed: Salespeople will almost always tell you that you look good in one of their gowns—they want your business. Isn't that why we like to bring our girlfriends and mothers to the store for support? Only those you are closest to can tell you that the dress of your dreams makes you look like the bride of your nightmares. So, at some level, it's helpful to reconceptualize wedding purveyors as an industry out to get your dollars.

And get your dollars it does. Couples tying the knot spend more than $20 billion a year on wedding ceremonies and receptions. But that's not all. They also spend $8 billion on honeymoons. And their friends spend $19 billion on gifts. That adds up to a lot of money, not to mention a lot of picture frames and bud vases. In fact, when all the math is done, nearly $50 billion is spent on weddings annually in the United States, though in researching this book I've seen estimates as high as $72 billion on such Websites as *theknot.com*. In other words, the wedding industry is estimated to generate as much as $72 billion in sales from wedding rings, wedding apparel, receptions, flowers, gifts, honeymoons, and other related expenses.

Now, of course, wedding businesses have a right to profit from their sales. After all, that is what America is all about. But being taken to the cleaners by these businesses is another matter. As consumers, we are especially vulnerable to wedding service providers for two reasons. First, the typical wedding negotiation is a one-shot deal. If all goes according to plan—and assuming we're not Elizabeth Taylor, Larry King, or Jennifer Lopez—we will have to rely on many of these retailers only once. That's one time for the florist, photographer, and caterer to get it right. Second, we are emotionally invested in our weddings. For some negotiations, such as, say, buying a used washing machine, we may be objective and rational. But when it comes to our own weddings, our heads may be a little in the clouds. We may not pay as much attention as we should to the details of various business transactions because we are in fairy tale mode. Or we may be too willing to compromise with unscrupulous service providers. In other words, we may be unusually prone to making basic errors in negotiation.

After all, a wedding is an incredibly expensive purchase, and too often we don't know how to do it right. So just as there are tips for purchasing a house, buying a car, and negotiating a job salary, there are proven strategies to help you negotiate your wedding. And, as Yoda from *Star Wars* might say, negotiate your wedding you should.

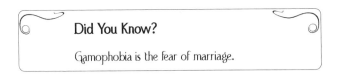

Did You Know?

Gamophobia is the fear of marriage.

So Who Am I?

This is where I come in. I am Shirit Kronzon, a negotiation scholar and member of the faclty at the Wharton School of Business at the University of Pennsylvania. There, for more than seven years, I have taught negotiation classes to executive businesspersons, management of business administration (MBA) students, and undergraduates. My course provides an introduction to the fundamental concepts of negotiation and offers strategies that can be used between individuals, companies, nations, and even among folks planning a wedding. How do I know? Because I am writing this book not just as a negotiation instructor, but also a newlywed. (If you haven't sent a gift, there's still time!)

I am ably assisted in writing this book by my long-time collaborator and friend, Andrew Ward. Like me, Andrew has a Ph.D. in psychology, and he is a faculty member at Swarthmore College. In addition, he has served as Associate Director of the Stanford Center on Conflict and Negotiation and is currently a faculty affiliate of the Solomon Asch Center for Study of Ethnopolitical Conflict at the University of Pennsylvania. For more than 15 years, Andrew has conducted research on negotiation, and he will be sharing his knowledge and expertise in this book. I can also tell you that he performed admirably in his recent role as "Guy of Honor" (what else does a bride call her male friend who helps out so much at her wedding?), offering a memorable toast, not to mention a song that brought the house down! I am happy to have him on board.

In my class I emphasize that negotiation is both a skill that needs to be developed and practiced, and a tool that can be used in a variety of settings. In the past, I have offered my students examples of negotiation concepts drawn from the fields of history, business, current affairs, and interpersonal relationships. But as I was planning my nuptials, I realized that, for each concept I discussed with my students, I could envision a relevant example taken from my own experience in planning a wedding.

So then it hit me: Brides, in particular, could benefit from a crash course on negotiation. If you think about it, you'll realize that all of wedding planning boils down to a series of discussions with various vendors—that is, a series of negotiations. When I researched the literature to find what wedding books mentioned about negotiation, the best I could generally find was this familiar piece of advice: Get it in writing. When it comes to business arrangements involving large sums of money, most of us understand that it's a good idea to receive a written contract. We know that we should review the contract. We may even know that we can edit it before we sign. But how do we negotiate the *terms* of that contract?

For example, when buying a gown, how do we negotiate any customized alterations to the dress? How do we bargain for an earlier delivery date? How do we guard against the additional charges that inevitably arise on our bill? When choosing a photographer, to take another example, we probably know that a contract should include the start and end time of the job, the number of proofs we will be permitted to receive and view for the final order, the size of the complete album, and maybe even some written assurance indicating how long prints will be available at a particular price. But how do we arrange it so that the prints are available for longer than the photographer specifies? Or how do we negotiate for more prints at the same price? In this book, I will help you to answer all these questions and many more.

Who said crushes never last?
Two out of five people have married their first love.

Who Are My Readers?

This book is for brides, grooms, and their families who want to hire professionals for their wedding. Consider these statistics: Every year an average of 2.5 million weddings occur in America. That's five million brides and grooms who get married every year in the United States alone. Today's median age for first-time brides is 25 years. For grooms, it's age 27. And, of course, second weddings are common—and not just among Hollywood celebrities. The median age for remarriage is 34 for women and 37 for men. My point here is simply that weddings take place throughout life. Indeed, 90 percent of women will be married at some point in their lives. That means that eventually just about every woman will be planning her wedding, and many will be helping others, such as their sisters, friends, or daughters, to plan nuptials— sometimes whether they want that help or not! Add to that grooms and families, all of whom may at some time or another find themselves involved in wedding preparations, and you'll begin to get a sense of the importance of having a guide to wedding negotiations that anyone can use.

Did You Know?

February 10th is World Marriage Day.

Apparently the 14th was already booked.

What's Out There?

Certainly there are a lot of books out there instructing you on how to cope with weddings. Go to any bookstore and you will find shelves of helpful advice on getting married. You will discover wedding planners that include worksheets, checklists, and calendars to help you organize your schedule. There will be books devoted to wedding courtesy and etiquette, which instruct you on everything from wording invitations correctly to knowing whether you really have to invite your future husband's best friend from high school. (Answer: You do, but you don't have to tell him about the open bar.)

You will also see books that focus on specific aspects of a wedding. For example, there are books that instruct you on how to write wedding vows, what counts as the world's greatest proposal, and who should give wedding speeches and toasts (best not to include anyone who majored in protoplasmic physics). There are books dealing with wedding showers, how to involve bridesmaids, where to take your honeymoon, and about religious and interfaith weddings. Look a little further and you will find creative guides to personalizing your wedding: for example, how to hold a vintage wedding or second wedding, or even an "anti-wedding"—whatever that is.

To be sure, there are books out there devoted exclusively to the topic of saving money on a wedding. Take a look and you will see that many of these books instruct the reader on how to save money by cutting corners from an ideal wedding, rather than using negotiation skills to get an ideal wedding at an affordable price. For example, what if you don't want to hold your wedding on a Tuesday afternoon in January in Point Barrow, Alaska? What if you don't want to invite family and friends by having them log on to *cheapweddinginvitations.com*? And what if you don't want to process down the aisle in a dress tailored by your great aunt with astigmatism while holding flowers that look like the ones your six-year-old niece made out of tissue paper in first-grade art class? In short, many suggested ways for saving money on a wedding are helpful, but at their core is the assumption that spending less money means compromising your preferences. I say, why compromise? Why not get the wedding of your dreams without having to settle for less than what you really want?

This book is *the* one and only primer to guide you through the journey of wedding negotiations. I will teach you the basics of bargaining and show you how to apply them in the context of your own wedding. I'll describe the common tactics that vendors use to get more money out of you, and I will give you hands-on negotiation advice that will not only help you defend yourself against their nefarious ways but will aid you in getting the best deals possible. I will go where no wedding advice book has gone before and explicitly tell you what words to say, phrases to use, and tone to take in bargaining with wedding service providers.

In short, using this book, you will develop successful negotiation strategies to help you plan your upcoming wedding. But there is no need to stop there: You can visit and revisit these skills in all the different negotiations you will encounter throughout your marriage. So here's wishing you a happy and long-lasting marriage! Let's begin....

Typical Costs of a Wedding in the U.S.
based on 175 guests
(Adapted from *theknot.com*)

Item	%	Expense
Gown	5	$1000
Ceremony	3	$600
Caterer	48	$9600
Cake	2	$500
Music	8	$1600
Photography	8	$1600
Videography	5	$1000
Flowers	8	$1600
Invitations	3	$600
Miscellaneous (transportation, lodging, etc.)	10	$2000
Total	100	$20,100

Chapter One

Negotiation

Most couples need be engaged for only a very short time before the questions begin: When are you planning to get married? Where would you like to hold your reception? Do you already have a color scheme in mind? How did you two meet? Does he have a brother? No doubt your mother, grandmother, aunt, sister, or best friend has peppered you with questions. In fact, I bet nearly every woman you've told about your engagement has had some question for you—men, too, but let's not count questions such as, "What's he got that I haven't got?" (money, a job, hair, lack of a criminal record—there are so many answers, really). And as you start formulating some rough answers to the myriad of (legitimate) questions, your parents (if they are going to help foot the bill) are undoubtedly asking themselves. The biggest question of all: What's this wedding going to cost?

You mean I have to pop the question more than once?
Only 4 percent of grooms ask the parents' approval
for their bride's hand.

Ah, the questions, the questions. In some ways, wedding preparations are merely answers to questions—some appropriate ("What would you like to serve at the reception?") and others, not so much ("Can I invite my cousin's best friend's dog groomer?"). As you begin to answer these questions, you are setting the foundation for planning your wedding day—planning that involves dealing with caterers, reception hall managers, photographers, florists—the list goes on and on. And along the way you'll have lot of questions for those various wedding service providers ("How much will this cost? Can we substitute this instead?"). In reality, answering many of those questions involves a kind of negotiation. You might not think of it as such, and that's okay, because many people shudder at the idea of formal negotiating. I'm here to take the pain out of it and show you that "negotiation" is just a slightly more systematic way of describing what you've probably already been doing. So, before you plunge headlong into wedding planning, I encourage you to relax, take a deep breath, and learn a little bit about the art and science of dealing with these folks. That is, the art and science of *negotiation*.

Negotiation: What You Do Every Day

I understand that, for many people, the subject of negotiation brings to mind an adversarial approach in which one person wins and the other one loses. For you, maybe the word conjures up images of sleazy car salesmen bent on scamming you. Or maybe it's that awkward conversation with the boss in which you ask for a raise. But when you get right down to it, negotiation is basically about making decisions.

Sometimes when we make decisions, we do so completely on our own. For example, an hour ago I made the decision as to what kind of lunch I wanted to have. After considering some available options, I decided to go for a cheese steak (after all, Philadelphia, where I live, is famous for those). So I made the decision, had full control over the outcome, and was quite satisfied with the result (heck, Philly wasn't named the "Fattest City in America" by specializing in sprouts and tofu).

Although I made this decision all by myself, I could just as easily have made it with someone else present. For instance, if I were meeting my co-author, Andrew, for lunch, we would have to decide together where to eat. He might want to go to one place—usually a diner ("What's wrong with a diner, Shirit?")—whereas I might be more inclined towards a different place, maybe a Middle Eastern restaurant ("You can't get hummus at most diners, Andrew!"). If that's the case, and, believe me, it has been the source of many discussions, the outcome (that is, where we eat) doesn't just depend on me, but it also depends on Andrew. It's only after we discuss it, that we make the decision and head to lunch, which usually turns out to be a nearby diner that does in fact serve hummus.

In formal terms, when I made the lunch decision alone, I made it independently. But if I make it with Andrew, I make it interdependently (what scholars refer to as "interdependent decision-making"). Negotiation is simply two (or more) people making decisions together.

When both parties want the same thing, it can go very smoothly ("I'd like to try that new pizza place." "Great—I've been wanting to try that place, too!"), assuming of course that what both parties want isn't a severely limited resource. ("I'm sorry folks, but our new pizza restaurant has room for only one more customer.") But when they have different preferences, things can get a little tricky ("I'm really in the mood for Mexican tonight." "Really? I was hoping for Chinese"). In the case of negotiating with Andrew, if I "lose," the worst that happens is that I end up eating a meal at a place I may not love. And, I admit it, hummus or not, I'm not a fan of Andrew's favorite diner.

In the context of wedding planning, however, the stakes are higher, and the parties' interests can be dramatically incompatible. Many wedding vendors want to milk you for every drop, and I think it's safe to assume you'd like to remain financially solvent. Add to that the fact that sometimes your interests may be incompatible with your own family's (or at least your future in-laws') desires for your big day, and you can see how useful good negotiation skills can be.

The Basics of Bargaining

As you go about planning your special day, you'll be setting up lots of meetings with various wedding professionals. These meetings serve several purposes: to discuss possibilities for your wedding, to look at samples, to find out whether what you want is actually available for your wedding, and, we must never forget, to find out how much everything costs. Let's get you ready for those meetings.

Whether it's with the florist or photographer, caterer or DJ, each meeting is likely to feature you and/or your representative, such as your fiancé, mother, or best friend, and the vendor. In many ways, your interests are diametrically opposed: You want to pay less for something; the vendor wants you to pay more. But you also share an interest: Assuming you like what the vendor is selling and assuming the vendor's good or service is actually available for your wedding, you both have an interest in reaching a deal. So, while your primary goal is to try to minimize the money you spend and the vendor's is to maximize it, both of you, to some degree, have a joint interest in actually transacting business with each other. What that means is that each side is probably willing to be a little flexible. You're willing to spend somewhat more than your absolute bottom line, and the vendor is willing to part with a good or service for a little less than if he or she had no interest in actually selling to you. And that means there is probably more room to negotiate than folks generally realize.

They hadn't even ventured outside the hotel room yet.
The length of an average honeymoon vacation is one week.

Now, to be sure, price is not endlessly negotiable, so it's always good to keep in mind a threshold—the absolute maximum you're willing to pay. And it's good to be aware of your alternatives—if, for example, there are a lot of other wedding gowns that appeal to you, you can stick to your guns and demand an attractive price on the one that has currently caught your fancy. If you get it at that price, great! If you don't, well, you have lots of options. You can offer up to your threshold or continue shopping. Of course, if you have few options, then your bargaining power is more limited, but you don't have to announce that fact. When Andrew bought his last car, he didn't mention that he currently didn't own one, had just moved to a new city without good public transportation, and was in desperate need of new wheels fast. Instead, when the salesman asked what he was currently driving, Andrew simply pointed to his rental car. (Fortunately he wasn't asked if he wanted to trade it in!)

Now the other problem is that you typically don't know what various vendors' options are. Are they desperate to sell? How much can they discount? Will they be offended if I try to negotiate? Obviously, there are no simple answers to those first two questions, and shortly I'll show you how you can negotiate even if you can't answer either. Regarding that last one, I have two answers. First, if you are worried about negotiating with a vendor, don't frame it in your mind as a negotiation. Frame it as a question—you are simply asking a question to see if a lower price is available. If you don't ask, you may never find out. Second, if a vendor gets offended by such a question, then that is probably not someone you want handling your wedding, and you have found out something important through asking your question. So even if the wedding service provider offers no discount and, in fact, becomes enraged at the mere suggestion of negotiating the price for a good or service, you have still gained something of value—you have learned that it's time to shop around some more.

> *Just to be safe, better make sure your best man is already married.*
>
> In a recent poll, American men and women were asked if they would marry the same person if they had it to do all over again. Eighty percent of the men responded that they would marry the same woman. Fifty percent of the women responded that they would marry the same man.

Who Should Make the First Offer?

Let's assume that you have decided to negotiate the price of something for your wedding—let's say the wedding cake. Should you wait until the baker tells you how much the cake costs and then offer something lower? Or should you preempt the process and make the first move, offering a price that is on the low end of your budget, but not ridiculously low? In the context of wedding planning, I strongly advise you *not* to make the first offer because, as I've suggested, you typically don't know much about the other side. You may not know, for example, how much wedding cakes typically cost, and thus you may offer a price that is far more than what the baker would be willing to accept. In domains in which you have little information, it's generally best to let the other side get the ball rolling. After all, even if you know nothing about the real cost of wedding cakes or the usual profit margin for bakers, one thing you do know is how much you are willing to spend on a wedding cake. If you are offered something above that threshold price, it may be time to find another baker.

Of course anytime that a vendor surprises you by asking for a price that seems exceedingly high, it pays to remember that he or she has a threshold, too—a bottom-line number representing the minimum acceptable price. How do you find out what that number is? Start by rejecting the first offer. There are several ways to do this. In general, I would go with the tactful approach:

"You're charging [X amount]? I see. Unfortunately that price is much higher than what I have budgeted for this."

In other words, make it clear that the vendor now faces a dilemma: lower the price or lose a potential customer. Under the circumstances, I think most vendors, especially if they aren't part of some huge conglomerate and therefore need most every customer they can get, will move to lower the price.

If you know of another vendor charging less, you can always add something such as the following:

"That price surprises me. You know that [Vendor Y] is offering pretty much the same package for far less."

Of course, if you have prior information, then making the first offer is not such a bad idea. For example, after you've read Chapter 5 in this book, you'll know that the national average for the cost of a wedding cake is typically $500 (of course in your area, the average price could be much higher—maybe even as much as $3000!). Coming up with your own number that is less than that does two things: It makes it likely that, if the other side accepts your number, you're getting a good deal; and, even if the other side doesn't accept your offer, it sets a reference point for subsequent negotiations.

> *At least he doesn't have to pretend that he's neat.*
> Statistics show that 75 percent of couples marrying
> today already share a home.

Reference Points

Imagine you decide to try a new restaurant in a resort area that you've never visited before. You take a look at the menu and see that almost every dish is between $25 and $35. You manage to find something on the menu for $22 and feel virtuous for ordering a relatively inexpensive meal. What you don't realize is that you could have had this same dish at the restaurant next door for $12.95 (of course the snooty waiter does cost extra, so maybe $22 is worth it to you). This is an example of reference points—when the average price of a meal is $30, $22 seems like a bargain. Expert negotiators know that if they can establish a reference point early in the proceedings, then even if you don't agree to their initial demand, you're likely to be bargaining in the ballpark of their price range, not yours. So whether you make the first offer or not, don't get sucked in by someone else's reference point. If someone says they can let you have a wedding cake for a mere $900, don't feel you have to come back with a "generous" offer of $850.

Did You Know?

It was the accepted practice in Babylon 4,000 years ago that for a month after the wedding, the bride's father would supply his son-in-law with all the mead he could drink. Mead is a honey beer, and because their calendar was lunar based, this period was called the "honey month" or what we know today as the "honeymoon."

What Do I Do Now?

No matter who ends up making the first offer, it is likely that agreement won't be reached right away. Don't worry—it's all part of the dance. Let's assume that you haven't opened with your absolute threshold price. And, indeed, in general it's not a good idea to start with an ultimatum-type price ("This is my final offer!"); it doesn't allow you to appear flexible, and let's face it, everybody—wedding vendors included—likes to think they can influence the other party in a negotiation. So, for example, imagine you are willing to spend up to $400 on a wedding cake, but you start by offering $300. If that offer is accepted, great! If not, offer subsequent concessions of smaller and smaller sizes—begin with something reasonable—maybe $50 ("Okay, I'm willing to pay $350"). If that doesn't do it, go with $25 ("All right. You talked me into $375"), then $10 ("I guess I can do $385). In that way, you signal to the other side that, although you are willing to be flexible, every subsequent concession you offer will be of a smaller and smaller amount.

Otherwise, if you offer the same concession every time—say $25 (for example $325, $350, $375, and so on)—the other side may get the idea to just wait and let you continue to offer that same amount indefinitely. Before you know it, you've worked your way up to paying $1000 for a cake—death by a thousand (cake) cuts. Similarly, there is no need to start with a huge concession ("You won't take $300? How about $600?"), which is likely to simply raise unrealistic expectations in the other party; or a tiny concession ("$300 is no good? How about $301?"), which won't be taken seriously. Finally, never make a unilateral concession. Any time you give up something, the other side should as well. Andrew knows that if he wants me to go to that lousy diner he likes so much, he's paying for my lunch! ("Gladly, Shirit!").

> ### Did You Know?
>
> Why is a wedding ring worn on the third finger? It was once believed that a vein of blood ran directly from the third finger on the left hand to the heart. The vein was called vena amori, or the vein of love, and early Egyptian writings on matrimonial procedure suggested that it would be appropriate for one's wedding ring to be worn on that special finger.
>
> *And yet somehow you never hear of anybody killing a vampire by stabbing him in the ring finger.*

Dirty Tricks

In each of the subsequent chapters of the book, I'll show you how to put into practice the negotiation fundamentals I've just reviewed. I'll also warn you about sleazy tactics that various vendors might use and show you how each gets played out in a particular setting, whether it's buying flowers or booking a reception hall. For now, let me just briefly overview some of these nefarious negotiation nonstarters.

> *It's okay to wear white.*
>
> Twenty-nine percent of women are virgins when they marry.
> *(How many claim they are?)*

Entrapment

Entrapment occurs when the other side gets you to commit to more and more resources to buy their particular product. You think you're going to spend, say $1500, on a wedding gown, and by the time all the hidden charges are added up (alterations, delivery, and so on), you're spending more than $2000. I'll show you how entrapment can happen in various domains relevant to your wedding and how you can avoid falling victim to it.

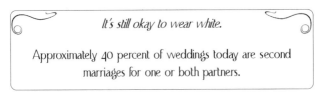

It's still okay to wear white.

Approximately 40 percent of weddings today are second marriages for one or both partners.

Liking

When you interact with wedding service providers, you're likely to make a lot of new friends, whether you want to or not. They'll compliment you and your taste, share their own wedding stories, reveal personal details, try to get you to do the same—anything to increase the chances that you identify with and like them. Because then you are more likely to buy whatever it is they are selling. And remember, as nice as they may seem, in the end they want to sell you something. Should you buy it? Maybe yes, maybe no. I'll help you separate the good feelings that come from having someone say nice things to you from those that come from getting a good deal on a prized wedding service or product.

Did You Know?

On average, a woman will speak 7000 words over the course of a day while a man will speak only 2000 words in the same period of time.

Bait and Switch

You're all ready to buy that beautiful gown in the shop window or that fabulous cake on the bakery display shelf. You reach for your wallet, only to hear that that particular product isn't available, but something comparable is, for just slightly more. As we'll see, you're likely the victim of bait and switch. Unfortunately, you've already persuaded yourself—and maybe others—that you're going to buy something—will you back out now? Chances are that you won't: Commitment is a powerful force. But maybe you should—I'll tell you when and how to do that.

They probably don't have TV remote controls.

The female lion does over 90 percent of the hunting. The male lion prefers to rest.

Deadline Pressures

Order before midnight tomorrow! You know the pitch. Deadlines make you feel like a good deal is about to evaporate, leaving you like Cinderella at 12:01 a.m.—so much for that princess gown you had your eye on. It's true that sometimes deals are limited in time, and it's good to pounce. But it's also true that many wedding vendors will use the threat of an impending deadline to get you to buy something that you don't need, can't afford, or could find for cheaper with a tad bit more searching. Don't get sucked in—I'll show you how to defeat this ploy and even use it to your own advantage. After all, a wedding vendor is not the only one who can invoke a deadline to get a good deal.

Nibbling

You think the deal is done. All the hidden charges have been explained, all the taxes and tips tallied, and it's time to settle up. You go to pay, when, oops, there's just one more tiny little charge that the wedding vendor forgot to mention. You're eager to have the whole matter resolved, so you agree to the extra charge even though you get nothing in return. If the negotiation were just starting, you would have demanded an equal concession from the other side (for example, "I'll pay the extra delivery charge, but I want a guarantee that it will be here by Wednesday."), but because the issue isn't raised until the end, the vendor gets something for nothing. Whether it's booking the reception hall or ordering a wedding cake, I'll show you how to take a bite out of nibbling.

Okay, now we're ready to negotiate. Let's go find a wedding dress....

Chapter Two

The Wedding Gown

Nothing symbolizes a wedding more than a bridal gown. Many brides-to-be scour dozens of bridal magazines, poring with great zeal over the glossy pictures, searching for the perfect dress. Even some single women I know have confessed to me that on occasion they sneak a peak at a bridal publication and, just for a moment, fantasize about how they would look in that Vera Wang number on their special day. Beyond ogling over dresses, brides sometimes go on extreme diets to make sure they'll look perfect in a gown that, at times, can feel like it was custom-made for the thinner sister of waif model Kate Moss.

Did You Know?

The 19th century marked the beginning of the Evil Bleach Industry Conspiracy.

Traditionally, European brides did not wear white wedding gowns. Through the 18th century, most brides just wore their Sunday best to their wedding.

Let's face it: Your wedding day is the day in which you get to look like a princess—or at least feel like one—but do you have to spend a king's ransom to do it? No! (Unless you really are a princess and your father really is a king, in which case you should probably stop reading this book and get on to more important matters, such as deciding which kind of caviar to feed the royal poodle at snack time). In short, in the serious quest to buy the perfect wedding gown, we often fail to consider that serious negotiations are involved, and how you fare in these negotiations can mean the difference between Yves Saint Laurent and "Don't miss our amazing closeout on slightly used, irregular 'dresses' that look and feel so good you hardly notice the smoky odor!"

Entrapment

Let's say you're standing inside a local bridal boutique. A saleswoman wanders over to you and asks if she can help. "Sure," you say, "I am looking for a gown for about $1000 dollars." "Great!" replies the saleswoman, gesturing dramatically, "I have just the thing!" And, indeed, to your left and to your right you see racks of potential gowns. Oh, where to start? You dive in right in the middle, and after a few minutes of pushing and pulling the heavy dresses, you find a few that catch your eye.

The saleswoman rushes over with excitement and then off you two go to the fitting room to try them on. One gown looks okay and is marked at an "affordable" $750. Another is a bit better and a wee-bit more at $1000. But the third dress is just gorgeous. As you stand there gushing at how pretty you look (okay, it's the saleswoman who's actually gushing, but who are you to argue?), you check the price tag: $1500. Uh-oh. That's a bit more than you had intended to spend. Oh, but it's so much prettier than the other dresses, not to mention your sister's—the younger sister who had the audacity to get married two years before you. "We don't have to decide right now," says the helpful saleswoman, as if she can read your mind. "If you really like that dress, let me show you a few more in a similar style." Why not? After all, you are the bride: you deserve it! So now you try a few more dresses and find one you *really* like—for $2000. "It's only $500 more than the other dress" you think to yourself as you look at yourself in that stunning gown and as the saleswoman and now her two assistants gush so much you begin to wonder if the store's ventilation system has malfunctioned.

> *And how many silkworms gave their life for the event?*
>
> Four hundred fifty yards of silk and lace were used to make Grace Kelly's wedding gown for her 1956 marriage to Prince Rainier of Monaco.

Stop for a moment. There is a danger lurking here: As you try on more and more dresses, you are also considering purchasing more and more expensive dresses. You have all but forgotten your "budget" price of $1000. How did this happen? This is called *entrapment*, the notion that as we get more and more involved in the search for something, we find we are willing to spend more and more to have it. You never would have considered buying a $2000 dress the moment you walked into the store; now, after 2 1/2 hours and enough salesperson gushing to fill the Goodyear blimp, it's hard to consider not buying it.

Here's another example. Imagine it's a few months later. By now you have decided to take the plunge and buy the $2000 dress, especially after seeing your sister's jaw drop when you told her about it, and you've come back to the store for a fitting. As you stand in front of the mirror looking at yourself, the tailor comes around to check the fit and secure some of the fabric with pins for further alterations. While these measurements are taken, the saleswoman asks you if you have thought about how you'll do your hair for the wedding. "Not yet," you say, but given that you have some time while the tailor is busy measuring the bustle behind you, it sounds like a fine idea to try some hair pieces. And so you find yourself trying hair clips, necklaces, even a tiara that you never thought you liked, and soon an accessory or two starts to feel like a real possibility.

Danger! While you came to the store ostensibly for a fitting, the store saleswomen had another agenda: specifically, to get you to buy accessories—anything from the veil, shoes, and gloves, to jewelry, a bra and pantyhose, even a guestbook. There is pressure to get everything right then and there from that store. Never mind that you could get those $200 shoes at a local department store for $50.

Why do salespeople do this? Quite simply, because they work on commission. They make money if they sell you a dress, any dress. But the higher the price of the dress, the more money they make. So they may steer you toward more expensive gowns. Once the gown is purchased, they turn to the accessories. Why sell you just a veil, when they can sell you a veil, shoes, and that tiara that makes you think you're Cinderella? Never mind that nowadays it's hard to get Cinderella's "just return everything by midnight and it's free" deal.

How to Handle It

"Untrap" Entrapment

Collect the data. Many of us may have spent years fantasizing about the gowns we'd wear. But when the time comes to really choose a dress, who knows if that particular style is actually flattering? Does what we imagined in our fantasy work in reality? Or maybe we don't have an inkling of what type of dress would look good, so we scan countless magazines and even surf Websites. But how will that dress in the magazine or Website actually look on us? After all, does a dress that looks good on an airbrushed, anorexic model really look good on an actual human being?

To find out, we have to be like a scientist and collect data. A white lab coat, however, is optional. We have to try on many dresses in many styles by many designers in many stores. Why? So that we understand that a princess cut makes our waist look smaller, or that tulle fabric makes our face look redder, or that an A-line cut frock by Amsale will cost $2500 to $3900. In other words, we need to know what dresses are available at what prices. In that way, we can avoid being lured into purchasing higher and higher priced dresses. As any nego-tiation expert will tell you, the key to successful bargaining is preparation.

To be sure, some stores let brides look through their en-tire dress selection before deciding which dresses they'd like to try on. And I recommend doing just that. Try on different styles at the first few shops you go to and get a feel for what accentuates your figure, for a style that could work. However, beware of stores in which they let you try only a handful of dresses. At one establishment, I was told that this was "store policy." I had to persist to get them to let me try an additional dress, apparently risking national security by violating their policy. Watch out, too, for saleswomen who first ask you to describe what you want and then bring it to you. On many occasions, the saleswoman will bring out dresses that *she* thinks are good for you, but can you trust her judgment? Does she really know you and your style intimately? Maybe the dresses she selects are the pricier ones that yield the store the most profit. Particularly because saleswomen know that first im-pressions make a difference, often the dresses they initially show you are, quite simply, the ones they most want to sell you—that's it, pure and simple. Indeed, I've been to stores where it's nearly impossible to get the sales staff to show me anything else. At one store I was even told that the only way to find out who designed a particular dress was to purchase it, at which point the designer's name would show up on the receipt. Needless to say, I didn't buy the dress, and I didn't go back to the store.

The key, then, is to first try on different styles of dresses, taking note of the typical price range for each. From there you can narrow down your choices to a specific style. Then you can take a second go at dresses in that style at various shops. And if, at that point, the salespeople insist on showing you something different, leave immediately—or maybe hand them a copy of this book and then leave.

Liking and Flattery: "You Look Like a Princess!"

I first observed this phenomenon when I served as Maid of Honor for my friend Denise. As a member of the bridal party, I was happy to accompany Denise on several wedding dress excursions, and Denise dutifully tried on dresses wherever we went. For every dress she tried, the salespeople had a compliment to offer. I began to wonder whether, if she wore a brown bag over her body, they'd gush "Ooh, the color compliments your skin!"

This flattery was particularly peculiar to me because, as her close friend, I couldn't find something nice to say for every dress. I debated with myself: How could I tell Denise that I didn't like a particular dress when it seemed that I was the only one in the room who didn't care for it? With at least two salespeople at any given moment oohing and aahing over every dress Denise tried on, there was a lot of pressure not to say anything negative. After all, maybe I would seem ill-intentioned when all I wanted to do was save Denise from making a mistake. Well, to make a long story short, after quietly pondering what I should do, I decided that I didn't want Denise to fall prey to the excessive fawning, and so I told her, in the most delicate words I could find, that "while the saleswoman simply loves the dress you have on, I think we can find one that complements you just a little better." This required some strategic planning to seize the one moment in which Denise was left unattended; thankfully, I wasn't forced to enact Plan B, which involved pretending to smell a natural gas leak. I'm happy to report that Denise didn't hit me and wound up getting a beautiful gown at half the price.

Did You Know?

Today, prior to a Jewish wedding ceremony, it is the groom who ritually "veils the bride." The reason for this tradition goes back to the marriage of Jacob to Leah (the older sister) when he thought he was marrying Rachel (the younger sister) whom he loved.

That must have been an interesting honeymoon.

A year later, when it came my turn to shop for dresses, I made sure to bring someone objective who could stand up for me like I had stood up for Denise. I strongly recommend this action. You may think that in bringing your family and friends, you've taken good precautions. But often you'll find that these folks are hesitant to say anything negative. So don't just gather your three closest gals and head to the bridal boutique. Make sure to tell them in advance that while the dress-trying-on process is just fun-beyond-belief, you would appreciate honest, constructive criticism. The goal here is not simply to bring an outside perspective to the shopping experience; you have to designate individuals to play the role of devil's advocate, that is, make them accountable so that they don't lose sight of what you've asked them to do.

So "assign" a friend to tell you what she likes as well as what she does not like about each dress you try on. Ask a second friend to record these observations and maybe even sketch some gowns so that you can remember each dress as well as your impressions of it at a later point in time. This process lets you visit and revisit the gowns at will, as you engage in careful decision-making. Particularly because gown stores typically do not let brides photograph dresses (that is, until you've shelled out money for the gown), it is essential that you be methodical in your gown-hunting experience (or get one of those cell phones that lets you secretly take pictures, but you didn't hear that from me). My point here is that without these preparations, there is just too much inherent temptation for observers to simply coo over how wonderful a bride looks in every dress she tries on, even if some make her look like the bride of Frankenstein.

> The tradition of having members of the wedding party dress alike was started in the hope that evil spirits would become confused and have a more difficult time distinguishing which one is the bride, and thus be prevented from putting a hex on her.
>
> *Let's hope the photographer was not equally confused.*

How to Handle It

1. Find Alone Time With Your Dress

There would be less temptation to succumb to the compliments if we, the brides-to-be, were given some time to look at ourselves alone in the dress. Instead, salespeople help us get into the dress, they walk with us to the mirror, they are there as we preen in front of it, and then they come back with us to the fitting room to take off the gown, where the process starts all over again. It's as if all of the wedding gown personnel in the world conspired to make us regress back to our child-hood! But we're not five years old. We are grown women on the brink of marriage no less—we can manage to look at our-selves in our gowns without having to hold the salesperson's hand (crossing a cobblestone street in three-inch heels is a different matter altogether). The salespeople, however, rarely like to leave us alone. Why is that? It's not as if we are likely to steal the dress. After all, it's pretty hard to fit a wedding gown under a jacket, even if you're Winona Rider.

Handle this obstacle by calmly insisting on a few personal minutes with the dress. You can indirectly request this time by saying something like the following:

> *"Perhaps you'd like to help that other customer for a moment while I consider the dress?"*

or more directly state,

> *"Thank you for your help. I'd appreciate it if you could give me a few minutes to consider the dress by myself."*

If nothing else works, pretend to spot a shoplifter on the other side of the store—just make sure that your mother isn't actually standing over there (oops, sorry Mom!).

2. Use a Ratification Strategy

You should not get swept away by the false compliments lavished on you. As noted earlier, make sure you bring some-one objective to help you choose a dress. Stress to your mother, sister, or girlfriends that you would truly appreciate an objec-tive opinion (at least about the dress—the time has past for "how can you marry him?" sort of advice). And if all else fails, bring a cell phone and call someone from the gown store. Even if you can't reach them, you can pretend to engage in a conversation in which your fiancé or family member does not approve of purchasing the dress.

This cell phone example illustrates a concept called *ratification*. You want to ask yourself whether ratification is required for the deal. That is, do you have to get permission from someone else before making the purchase? You can use the need for ratification to strengthen your position, by noting to the saleswomen that the ratifying figure, such as your fiancé or family, does not grant you the authority to purchase the dress. Moreover, you can use this ratification ploy to squeeze out an extra concession in order to have "the boss" approve the deal. For example, you can indicate to the salesperson that only if the price of the gown is reduced by $300 will your fiancé or family approve the purchase.

Bait and Switch

Let us suppose that you have fallen in love with a gown you saw in a bridal magazine. You call the number listed in the advertisement and make arrangements to try on the dress. The day you arrive for your appointment with the picture of your dream dress in hand, the store representative surprises you by claiming that the store does not "happen to have" that particular design, but they do have another dress just like it.

Or let us assume that you have already ordered a wedding gown. You put some money down. Months pass. Finally, you get a call from the wedding gown saleswoman who excitedly informs you the dress has arrived at the gown store! You promptly cancel all of your appointments and make a mad dash to the store to finally be betrothed to your gown. Because let's face it: By this point in the months-long wedding preparations process, you feel just about as engaged to your wedding gown as to your fiancé. To your dismay, you immediately notice that the fabric of the dress is different from what you had ordered. Such a scenario happens all too often. Brides enter the store giddy with glee that after months of waiting for it to arrive, they can finally see their own dress, only to find that the fabric has been changed, the trim is different, or the lace is cheaper than was advertised.

What is going on here? The infamous *bait-and-switch strategy*. The gown store *baits* you with an advertisement of an attractive dress and then *switches* the dress for another that is of lesser quality or more expensive or both. Or the store lures you into ordering a particular gown only to deliver a different dress. In many cases, individuals reluctantly agree to the switch.

Why do people go along? Because people like to be consistent. Once you have gone through the trouble of choosing a dress and committing to buy it, inertia sets in and we do everything we can to rationalize your decision, even if that means accepting something less than perfect. Especially when it comes to important decisions, once you decide to act, it can be almost impossible to restrain yourself, even if there are good reasons to do so. As Isaac Newton said, bodies in motion tend to stay in motion—and he wasn't even trying to buy a wedding dress when he said that.

And you thought it was the British they were fighting.

During the American Revolution, many brides did not wear white wedding gowns; instead, they wore red as a symbol of rebellion.

And psychedelic purple meant it was time to switch to non-alcoholic punch.

Other colors were worn for symbolic reasons: blue meant constancy and green meant youth.

Clever negotiators can exploit our tendency to want to be consistent by initially providing strong incentives for us to act. They know that, after the decision has been made to buy a dress, we are likely to increase our commitment to it. We think about how much we love the gown and sometimes invent new reasons for why the dress is perfect ("Hmm. I'm just noticing how much the dress accentuates my thin calves"). Here's where the glitch occurs: After you've made the decision to buy the dress, but just before the deal is sealed, the seller removes the inducement. Like when the store "magically" no longer carries the dress that they just advertised! Or when the store offers us a different dress than the one we ordered. Removing these inducements should suggest that we need to re-think the purchase, but our decision to buy a dress frequently stands firm. It's as if our commitment has a life of its own. After engaging in a drawn-out negotiation, we don't want to ruin the deal and/or jeopardize the relationship we have built with the staff, so when we are told the dress is not available, we see what else the store has to offer. Or when we are informed that our dress has been changed in some way, we buy it anyway.

How to Handle It

1. Find Out If the Other Side Is Trustworthy

Try to determine before the negotiation how faithfully the other party typically lives up to its commitments. Ask friends or relatives who have dealt with the store in the past about their experiences: Does this store have a reputation for honesty or might it substitute one dress for another? Does it advertise a certain dress but then have only one in the store, size 0? What is the store staff prepared to do if they can't deliver the dress they promised? How often does that happen? Ask such discerning questions of others who have been through the wedding "wringer" already and are in the know. This might even involve asking your future father-in-law's sister's daughter's best friend for her impressions. And remember that if you have not heard positive things about a store or you do not feel comfortable dealing with the staff, feel free not to purchase a gown from that location. Some business is just not worth the trouble it becomes.

2. Prepare, Prepare, Prepare

By determining before the negotiation precisely what the other party's real needs and wants are, and what problems might come up later, you can anticipate possible changes in your terms. For example, when I was in the process of buying my wedding gown, I was concerned that it would not be ready in time for the ceremony, particularly because the gown was being shipped from Europe. In order to allay this fear, I noted on the contract that, should the gown not make it to my wedding in time, I would be entitled to the store sample of my dress—which the store owner had been reluctant to sell, as it was prominently displayed in the store window and, presumably, lured customers into the store—at a greatly discounted price! Likewise, make your contract or agreement as detailed as possible. The more detailed it is, the fewer chances of misunderstandings between the store and yourself.

Nibbling

Imagine you're buying an expensive car. You go through a lengthy negotiation with the dealer, including two occasions in which he abandons you to speak to his "sales manager," who you're never sure really exists, but finally you agree on a price. You're just about to sign on the dotted line when, oops, he forgot to mention the $375 "delivery" charge. Never mind that you live in Michigan and you suspect that the car came from the auto plant down the street (this actually happened to a friend of mine). After negotiating a $44,000 purchase, another $375 seems like chump change. In a way, it is.

Nibbling describes a strategy of requesting a further small concession just before a deal is sealed. The nibbler raises an issue that, in and of itself, seems sufficiently trivial that, in the context of the whole negotiation, additional bargaining seems pointless. So the nibbler wins the concession without having to give up anything in return. As noted earlier, after engaging in a difficult and time-consuming negotiation in which a settlement at last seems at hand, most people do not want to ruin matters by quibbling over small potatoes, so they make unilateral concessions.

In the context of gown shopping, nibbling is used by salespeople who charge for such things as shipping and handling, either from the gown supplier to the bridal store or from the bridal store to your home, a protective gown bag, pressing, inflated alteration charges, and so on. This nibbling strategy works because brides often look at just the price of the gown, not knowing there may be additional costs involved in the purchase. And bridal store salespeople typically neglect to disclose to customers these add-ons until it is convenient for them to do so. In other words, you try on *the* dress, fall in love with it, and only after you've made the purchase do the saleswomen explain the extra charges that hike up the price.

To be sure, some charges make sense, such as rush delivery if you forgot to order your veil and find that it's a week before your wedding, or last-minute alterations because your pre-wedding jitters caused you to unexpectedly lose 10 extra pounds. In these instances, the additional effort should certainly be compensated.

But consider the case of my good friend's mother, who paid more than $1000 for her dress, an amount that is greater than many brides spend on their wedding gown! For that price she naively assumed that alterations would be included. Surprise! I was with her on the occasion that she learned that simple alterations to the sleeves of her dress would require an additional payment of $25. I repeat, $25. My friend's mother had spent an exorbitant $1000 for a dress, and yet the store refused to comp a $25 charge. Needless to day, she was livid. Livid but trapped. She found herself in a situation in which she had already shelled out the price of the dress, with the alterations process already underway. Unfortunately, she could not really walk away from the "bargaining table" without losing her large monetary investment. So what did she do? You guessed it. She paid the money.

This nibbling tactic nearly trapped me as well. Let's pick it up from the point in the negotiation where the store had received my wedding dress from the supplier and alterations were about to begin. The saleswoman was very vague about the precise number of fittings I was to receive to adjust my dress, and I logically assumed that her preference would be for the smallest number possible. So we made an appointment for the first fitting, that is, for me to try on the dress and for the tailor to assess just what exactly needed to be done. By the second fitting, progress had been made, and we noted that the shoulder straps of the dress did hold me tighter, as I had desired.

We next turned to the topic of the bustle of the dress. Measurements were taken and an appointment was set for fitting number three. When this fitting occurred, my mother discovered that the bustle had been sewn incorrectly. In fact, the dress had been sewn so as to be permanently bustled—so much for the dramatic entrance with my long train I had longed for. After heated discussions, new measurements were taken, and pins were inserted into the material—fortunately, given the circumstances, not into me! Now we were on to the fourth fitting. At last, after weeks of trials and tribulations, the dress finally fit perfectly. Here's the punch line: During this whole process of gown alterations, the saleswoman never once mentioned what this work would cost, which implied to me that alterations must be included in the price of the dress. But as that final fitting concluded, the saleswoman informed me that she now had to tally the cost of the alterations.

Pause here for a moment and let's think together. What should the saleswoman reasonably charge me? An amount based on the number of fittings? The hours of work on my gown? Clearly I did not wish to pay for the additional fitting or the hours of labor necessary to repair the tailor's bustle mistake. And I was never given an alterations chart detailing the cost or, for that matter, any information about alterations at all. In short, how was I to know that whatever amount the saleswoman wanted to charge me was fair or reasonable?

How to Handle It

1. Get It in Writing

My contract was my savior! In fact, six months earlier when the terms were drawn, the saleswoman agreed to insert a clause in the contract that alterations would be included for free. As it turned out, while I had been faintly aware of this clause throughout my fittings, my saleswoman's memory was not as sharp; thus, she attempted to charge me up the (incorrectly bustled) wazoo, or so it seemed.

A strong defense against nibbling, then, is to research all the possible charges that might arise somewhere down the road. Ask about these charges up front and record how they are to be resolved in a contract at the time of purchase, if not before. Get the receipt with the name of the dress or style number, designer, color (who knew that there were so many variants of white?), size (including all of the assorted measurements that were taken of you), delivery date, price, estimate of alteration costs, and shipping and handling charges. (Incidentally, does anyone actually know what "handling" charges are? I'd like for as few people as possible to handle my dress, thank you very much.) If, for example, the store recommends a particular size, record that fact on the receipt, because should you later find that that size dress does not fit you, the contractual burden is on the store to correct it.

It is also important to ascertain the store's refund policy. Ask what happens if the dress does not arrive or, God forbid, you have to cancel your wedding: how much will you have to pay? By the way, if you are thinking about canceling your wedding, you might employ this creative solution instead: A friend of mine broke up with her fiancé about five months before she was to get married in a wedding to rival Princess Diana's. Undeterred, she met someone else, got engaged, and went ahead with the nuptials as planned; after all, substituting the groom was a lot easier than getting the reception hall deposit back. I'm happy to report that today, several years later, they are still happily married with two lovely kids. All's well that ends well.

Understand the store's payment policy. That is, how much you have to put down at each stage of the process. Do not make a final payment until you obtain a completed dress; otherwise store employees will have little motivation to complete the dress, as they already have your money. Read carefully before you sign the contract, and amend it, initialing the changes, as necessary.

2. Invest the Other Side in the Negotiation

If you don't know your opponent, make sure the other party is just as invested as you are in the negotiation. The goal here is to make the store personnel want the sale just as much, if not more, than you do. If the store owner is desirous of your business, she may be less likely to spring unpleasant surprises upon you.

Toward that end, it may be wise to make the salesperson your friend. Talk to her about details of your wedding to make her feel included. For example, when I purchased my gown, but before I actually received it, I took pictures of the dress, and I included the owner of the store in several of the snapshots. In another instance, I brought along my friend who dutifully hit on the saleswoman (okay, I didn't actually tell him to do that—and he's still waiting for her to call). Throughout my visits to the store, I also stressed to the owner that I was planning to recommend the establishment to several friends who were soon-to-be-engaged. In all of these attempts, my aim was to foster friendly ongoing relations between the store associates and myself. I reasoned that a good relationship with the other party would reduce the likelihood that the store would take harmful actions against me and, more importantly, my wedding gown.

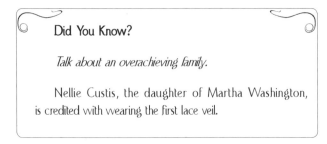

Did You Know?

Talk about an overachieving family.

Nellie Custis, the daughter of Martha Washington, is credited with wearing the first lace veil.

3. Insist on Reciprocal Concessions

Still, if you find that the other party is trying to nibble, do not panic. Just remember not to respond with an automatic "yes" to last-minute demands. Instead, realize that you have two options. The first is a conditional yes response. That is, saying something such as, "All right, I'll agree to what you want, if you also agree to what I would like to happen." Then spell out what you want in return. What you are doing, then, is insisting on a reciprocal concession.

For example, let's say that the store wants to charge you, as an afterthought, for shipping and handling, or a protective gown bag, or pressing, or inflated alteration charges, or _____ (fill in this blank as it applies to you). You respond with,

"That will be fine, as long as you can include at no charge my veil, shoes, gloves, bras, tiara and/or _____ " (again, fill in this blank as it applies to you).

In this manner, you do not allow new issues to be considered unless the other party is also willing to talk about other issues, even ones that you had previously agreed upon. If the other party wants to raise a new issue after everything else has been settled, then the entire contract should be open for renegotiation. So, should the saleswoman attempt to include an additional cost that is not already specified on your contract, tell her the following:

"Given that we already have a completed contract for the gown purchase, adding it or changing in such a way does not seem like a fair thing to do, unless we make amendments in my favor as well."

Deadlines

Their Deadline

Wedding gown stores often employ deadlines to their advantage, using what is termed the scarcity effect. All too frequently saleswomen admonish that the dress you happen to be fond of will be gone or discontinued or sold to someone else if you don't buy it now. Here's my experience with this shady strategy: When a store pressured me to buy a dress pronto or it would be gone tomorrow, I thought that perhaps I could compromise by leaving a small deposit as a gesture of good faith. The saleswoman dealing with me refused this token and instead handed me a receipt that stated that I had just paid this sum of money, even though I had not. This seemed peculiar to me, and as I further scrutinized the "receipt," I learned that it was in fact a contract that stated that, should I renege on the gown purchase, I would owe half the price of the dress! So what began as an innocent gesture to extend a deadline turned into an attempted ploy against me. Needless to say, I didn't purchase the dress.

As my example reveals, deadlines are a potent weapon in negotiation. A contract is about to expire....Someone is about to go out of town....Agreement must be reached before a high-level summit can take place. Deadlines affect us by invoking a sense of scarcity, creating the feeling that time is running out on some golden opportunity. And, as my experience shows, deadlines can be costly to you because you either have to try to extend the deadline or end up with nothing.

How to Handle It

1. Change the Schedule of the Negotiation

Should a gown store attempt to impose a deadline on you in order to get the sale, consider the option of changing the schedule of negotiations. Business people going abroad sometimes have bargaining sessions scheduled to begin right after their planes land, when they are still feeling the effects of jet lag. Rather than labor under these challenging circumstances, savvy individuals will often change the time of a negotiation to afford them the opportunity to nap and become refreshed for the upcoming business dealings.

Similarly, when looking at wedding gowns, you might calmly and confidently tell the salesperson the following:

"I understand that you are suggesting a deadline for when I should purchase the dress I am interested in. I will contact you in a couple of days when it is convenient for me to discuss purchasing it."

Because buying a dress involves such a large expenditure of money, in most cases, it is prudent to take time to consider the decision as well as to realize that the dress will probably still be available in a few days. So you can sleep on it. Don't wait weeks or months, but a few days is fine, unless you're in a store like Kleinfeld's in New York or Filene's Basement in Boston during their special bridal sales, at which dozens of women trying to knock you over to get to your dress should probably serve as a helpful hint that the deal won't be available tomorrow.

2. Invite Some Competition

Alternatively, you can impose a deadline on the store to sell you the dress at the price that you desire. For example, if the saleswoman pressures you to buy the dress today, match her "sense of urgency" by saying, "I will purchase the dress today if you can knock off $200." Realize that if it's a popular dress style, other places are likely to carry it or, at the very least, offer something similar. In fact, I recommend that you call these other places and find out if they sell such a style, if it is currently available, and what they are charging for it. Then, if necessary, you might also make mention of the competition. For example:

"How about I give you until the end of the week to offer me this dress at this price. After that, I'll be going to [your competitor] for the item."

A third option is to bring an objective person in with you (see the previous "Liking and Flattery" section). If all else fails, don't bring any money!

Your Deadline

Thus far we have discussed how to combat a store's attempt to invoke scarcity and deadlines to pressure you to purchase a wedding gown. Stores typically use deadlines both to convince you to buy the garment and to get you to pay the various portions of the bill on time. But once you commit to purchasing a dress, the store that previously seemed so concerned with deadlines can suddenly seem to takes its own sweet time and sometimes more than that to get things done. The major concern here is what happens if the dress is not ready on time?

Did You Know?

Mystique and romance has surrounded the veil for more than one thousand years. Brightly colored veils were worn in ancient times in many parts of the world and were considered a protection against evil spirits. Greek and Roman brides wore yellow or red veils to ward off evil spirits and demons.

The veil is thought to have been used to hide the bride from abductors or evil spirits, just as the similar dress of her bridesmaids was meant to do.

In early European history, with the advent of arranged marriages, veils served another purpose to prevent the groom from seeing the bride's face till after the ceremony was over. Brides began to wear opaque yellow veils. A more romantic interpretation evolved later which believed that concealment (as the bride's face beneath a veil) rendered what was hidden more valuable.

Another early interpretation of the veil was that it symbolized youth and virginity.

And yet another interpretation is that it symbolized a way to charge more money for a wedding dress.

How to Handle It

1. Give Yourself Some More Time

First, you can give yourself a little extra time. Tell a small fib and say that your wedding is sooner than it really is. If it is August 11, say July 11. That way, if the store delays a little, you're still okay. Make sure you fudge by only a month or two; otherwise you risk sounding not credible and/or a little too much like Glenn Close's character in *Fatal Attraction.*

2. Offer Incentives

You can offer the store incentives for meeting your deadlines. According to G. Richard Shell, author of *Bargaining for Advantage*, firms offering jobs to prospective employees will often give them deadlines to accept job offers and include terms such as cash bonuses and priority in selecting job sites if they accept by the deadline. If you are such a prospect, the overall job offer is still good after the terms disappear, but you miss out on extra benefits if you delay your decision. For example, a firm will often threaten to withdraw a particular perk if you don't act right away. In the same vein, you might write into your contract with the wedding store that you will pay for a storage bag if the dress arrives on time; if it doesn't, the bag is free.

3. Make the Deadline Real

Finally, don't be afraid to link deadlines to events in the outside world that parties do not control, for example certain holidays such as Christmas or New Year's:

"I'll need the dress by [insert date] because that is the only day that both my family and the photographer are available for prenuptial pictures."

Make deadlines credible: "I must have this dress six days after the vernal equinox" is probably not your best bet. Likewise, I'd avoid, "I need this dress by next Saturday because I told my boss that I'm getting married that day rather than attend an all-day seminar on ethics in the workplace." This one won't work for several reasons.

Summary

Let's recap how to counter the most common tactics used by zealous wedding service providers:

Entrapment

- "Untrap" entrapment by collecting information about wedding gowns and trying on many different styles.

Liking and Flattery

- Bring along a trusted family member or friend.
- Find alone time with your dress.
- Use a ratification strategy.

Bait and Switch

- Research the store ahead of time.
- Anticipate changes to the contract.

Nibbling

- Get the contract in writing.
- Invest the other side in the negotiation.
- Insist on reciprocal concessions.

Deadlines

- Change the schedule of the negotiation.
- Invite competition.
- Give yourself more time.
- Offer the store incentives.
- Make your deadline real.

Chapter Three

Ceremony *and* Reception

When planning your wedding, one of the first things you should do, after gloating incessantly in front of your still-single friends, is to book the location for the ceremony and the reception. Unless you are Tori Spelling, daughter of legendary television producer Aaron Spelling, who conveniently held her wedding at her dad's 56,000-square-foot Los Angeles mansion, you're going to want to shop around a bit. After all, even Tori's wedding ended up costing a reported $1 million dollars, so I guess holding it at her dad's house wasn't all that cost effective (especially when you consider that her husband filed for divorce a little more than a year later—that's a lot of money for 15 months of marriage). For us mere mortals, who don't have access to a free Hollywood mansion, we have to think about what kind of location we're interested in, how formal we want the wedding to be, and whether we have a theme or particular atmosphere in mind for the wedding.

I admit this task will probably be the most time-consuming of all of your wedding preparations—a challenge for many a newly-engaged couple. But it's important to visit different venues to get a sense of how you'd like your wedding to be. You might think about such places as outdoor gardens and parks, museums, country clubs, historic mansions, and of course, particular houses of worship.

> *Snow tends to mess up a wedding gown.*
> June is the most popular month for weddings, followed by
> August, September, October, and May.

When it comes to choosing a reception site, some locations, such as restaurants and country clubs, are, in wedding-speak, "on-site," meaning that the site includes most (if not all) of the amenities you need: food and beverage, tables and servingware, service staff, and so on. Other locations, such as a park or museum are "off-site," in which you rent the site and then must contract with various vendors to supply everything else for your reception. (For more on this distinction, see Chapter 4.)

Now if you happen to be like Star Jones, one of the co-hosts of ABC's *The View*, who, before getting married, mentioned repeatedly (and I do mean repeatedly) on the air that she had been planning her dream wedding since she was a child, then you already know everything you want, and all you have to do is order your fiancé to stay out of the way. But if you're like most people, you're going to want to take the time to investigate not just what you think you want, but what's available in the area where you'll be getting married. For me, a native Californian, getting married in Philadelphia meant a serious exploration of the area. It took a lot of time, yes, but it felt good to know what was actually available so that I could make the best decision.

When I looked around, sometimes I went alone, sometimes with a friend, and sometimes with my fiancé. To make the chore more enjoyable, every time my fiancé and I looked at a new place, we would get coffee or dinner afterwards as a reward for our diligence and hard work. In other words, we turned each exploration into a kind of date. So my advice is: When looking at places, have fun with it!

Did You Know?

Although most weddings now take place on a Saturday, it was considered unlucky in the past. Fridays were also considered unlucky for marriage ceremonies, particularly Friday the 13th.

You might still want to steer clear of Memorial Day.

Location, Location, Location

The Indoor-Versus-Outdoor Question

As you think about location possibilities, think about whether you'd like the ceremony and/or reception to be indoors or outdoors. If you plan to hold everything indoors, feel free to skip ahead to the next section. But if you plan to get married outdoors, obviously you must consider the weather. Given that I am from the beautiful sunshine-land of California, I knew I wanted an outdoor ceremony—no question. I mean, I'm not one of those crunchy granola types who like to backpack everywhere and think that the bride should process down the aisle to the lulling strains of Kumbaya ("Someone's marrying, Lord..."). But I knew I wanted at least part of my wedding to be outside. So I spent many afternoons visiting sites that specialize in or at least include an element of the outdoor ceremony. And I must confess that at first I was very disappointed with what I found.

For example, many places mislead you into believing that you will have an outdoor location when in reality you won't. Case in point: There's an expensive hotel in New Jersey that actually has the words "Seaview" in its name, which, call-me-crazy, I thought might mean that the place was you know, by the sea. In fact, even though their wedding literature features a picture of a beach, it turns out that the place is about a mile from the sea. They don't have a beach where you can get married, nor do they let you get married in the vast stretch of land that is sandwiched between the hotel and the sea. Other places I visited did include a beach or a garden but often their brochures made such locations look a lot grander than they were. When I visited one, for example, I discovered I could get married in their "garden," which was actually a small patch of grass stuck between a road and a swimming pool that was likely to be filled with screaming kids on the day of my wedding (believe me, if anyone's gonna be screaming on my wedding day, it had better be an ex-boyfriend). Still another place, a very expensive hotel in Philadelphia in fact, featured a garden that was fenced in on three sides by high walls, with the remaining side facing a major street. Granted the traffic noise could be useful in blocking out the ex's screams, but other than that, I wouldn't recommend the place.

Did You Know?

Bad weather on the way to the wedding is thought to be an omen of an unhappy marriage; some cultures, however, consider rain to be a good omen. Cloudy skies and wind are believed to cause stormy marriages. Snow, on the other hand, is associated with fertility and wealth.

And pneumonia.

Bait and Switch

These are all examples of bait and switch. You are lured by visions of, for example, a wedding on the beach, only to find out that the place doesn't actually offer a beach location. If, on the other hand, you are pleasantly surprised by what you find, by all means continue to consider that location. But don't feel pressure to choose the location if it turns out not to have what you really want.

Contingent Contract

Okay, let's say you've visited a site that has that outdoor garden atmosphere that you've been seeking. Good for you, but don't book the place just yet. You also need to make sure that it includes an indoor facility that will work in the event of inclement weather. Despite what Benjamin Zander, conductor of the Boston Philharmonic and co-author of *The Art of Possibility*, once said ("There's no such thing as bad weather; there's only inappropriate clothing!"), sometimes it does rain on your parade. This is what folks in the business world call a *contingency*, a condition that may occur. So if you are going to be married outside, you must prepare for the contingency of rain, unless, of course, it's the summer time in San Francisco—though in that case heed the warning of Mark Twain, who quipped that the coldest winter he ever spent was a summer in San Francisco! (okay, it turns out that he never actually said that, but anyone who has gone to San Francisco in the summertime expecting hot, sunny weather only to find cold, foggy drear can surely relate). Be aware that some places require advance notice before you can use their indoor facility. One bride I know was informed that she had to decide 48 hours before the event whether to hold it indoors or not—makes one hope the weatherman knows what he's talking about.

I recently attended a wedding in Utah in the Red Butte Botanical Gardens. The gardens were simply breathtaking, but it started to rain. The bride and groom insisted on remaining outdoors for the ceremony. I figure either they thought a miracle would happen and the rain would vanish or they didn't want both the ceremony and the reception to be indoors. Regardless, while we sat outside in the rain, they rushed through the ceremony so we could all get inside before it really poured. Don't let this happen to you. You should consider what is going to happen in case of bad weather on your day. For example, would you be okay getting married inside at the same location if the outdoor part of your venue is unusable?

This is important to consider because lots of places have stunning outdoor facilities but less-than-terrific indoor ones. When I was looking for a place, I remember my future mother-in-law suggesting a site that was conveniently close to her home and included a beautiful garden. I thought that the outdoor location was perfect, but the indoor option, in the event of rain, was a colonial-style mansion that just wasn't going to work for this California girl. Another location, an Arboretum in fact, was beautiful outside, but the inside looked like a cafeteria. And indeed, many of the outdoor locations I checked out were cursed with dilapidated indoor options.

In the end, the place I found for my special day was a golf club situated in a lovely Philadelphia suburb with a beautiful view of rolling hills and forests. But it also featured a surprisingly modern indoor facility, something that I had longed for but was starting to think might be impossible to find around stately old Philly. When I inquired about this seeming architectural anomaly, I learned that the golf clubhouse had burned down a couple of years back and had just been rebuilt anew. I'm sure this was most unfortunate for the country club owners, but it was oh-so fortunate for me. The moral of the story is that if you persist and look hard enough, coupled with a little luck, you can find your dream wedding site—something that will work both outdoors and, if need be, indoors, too. To this day my husband jokes, "Thank God for the fire!"

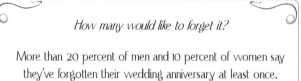

How many would like to forget it?

More than 20 percent of men and 10 percent of women say they've forgotten their wedding anniversary at least once.

I should also mention something about warm weather places. If you are going to have a ceremony outside, note the amount of heat you may have to put up with. For example, my in-laws are not fans of the sun (my father-in-law is a dermatologist), whereas my family consists of desert dwellers unaffected by heat. So we had a clear disagreement here. We solved it by integrative bargaining: My interest was in having an outdoor wedding. Their interest was in not sweating and sweltering in the August heat. So, we integrated our interests and agreed to an outdoor ceremony but one that was relatively brief, limiting the length of time guests would be in the heat to a more reasonable 30 minutes (Andrew was grateful for that: "Looking back, Shirit, I guess I shouldn't have worn a wool suit"). In particular, guests got to mingle in the air-conditioned indoors prior to the actual ceremony, then returned there for the reception. In between, I got to be outdoors for my beautiful ceremony—win-win to be sure.

Getting the Right Room: Another Case of Bait and Switch?

As you consider the reception hall, make sure that you are really going to get what you think you're getting. Sometimes reception site staff may try to set you up in a room that is different from what you anticipated. In other words, they employ bait and switch: They get you excited about a place and then only later reveal some deficiency in the setting.

For example, when I was planning my wedding, my in-laws took me to see a country club that, at least initially, looked great. However, it turned out to be the club I alluded to near the beginning of this chapter. That is, as I walked around the area, trying to envision where on the premises we'd hold the ceremony (as I recommend that you do too), I recognized that the space outdoors would require that the wedding be held by the pool. At first this was something that I did not really mind, despite the tight quarters that would be required because of a road that cut into the property at an awkward angle. Only at our next appointment did I find out that that the pool would be in normal operation during the ceremony! I mean, it's one thing to be married next to an empty, peaceful pool, which can actually add a touch of serenity to your ceremony. It's another thing entirely to be married next to toddlers splashing around, older men tanning themselves in Speedos, and a lifeguard who's trying to find a girlfriend.

When I pointed out this concern to the manager, she explained that members retained the prerogative to swim during my wedding; after all it was their club. Although she hoped that no one would be using the facility during the ceremony, she could not guarantee it. You know you're in trouble when you're left hoping that it rains up until the moment your wedding begins, just so you can be sure that no one will be using the adjoining pool!

After all, it's a gamble.

The number-one wedding city in the world is Las Vegas, with more than 100,000 weddings annually. Can you guess the second? Hawaii, with over 25,000 weddings.

Now, I understand that people pay a lot of money to join country clubs, and they should be able to swim during regular hours of operation. What I am opposed to is the club's plan to make additional money by moonlighting in the wedding business. As you too are spending lots of cash on your special day, like I said before, you shouldn't have to strain to say your vows over the noise of kids at the pool.

This phenomenon is not just restricted to country clubs with inconvenient pool schedules. I recall another country club I visited that was brand new. I remember walking around the site, marveling at the lush greenery, the manicured lawns, the stunning floral landscaping, the beautiful marble-adorned buildings. As the hostess took us on a brief tour, she let us take a quick peek at a room that featured floor-to-ceiling windows, affording a breathtaking view of the golf course outside. As I was imagining myself floating around the room, the harsh voice of the hostess broke my reverie to inform me that the room was to be used "only for members' private affairs." Okay, I said, and asked to see the room to be used for nonmembers' parties, hoping it would be just as grand. Let's just say that an apt analogy would involve a comparison between a premium deluxe suite in a five-star luxury hotel and the waiting room at the department of motor vehicles. Now let me ask you this: Wouldn't you feel a little bit uncomfortable with the notion of booking a less attractive room, while knowing that there is a spectacular room nearby that you're not allowed to use? I know I did. And I promptly left the country club.

I urge you to pay careful attention to the setting of your wedding. Watch out for unexpected sources of noise: kids by the pool, highway noise, or folks having dinner in the room next to your reception site in a restaurant. For instance, will your wedding location be next to a parking lot or just off the first tee on a golf course, as in some sites that I have seen? Now I realize this can all be okay (after all, that's why you have a florist: to disguise some imperfections of the location), as long as you stipulate in your contract that there will no significant distractions during your ceremony. Before my husband met me, he attended a relative's wedding in which the sprinklers suddenly went off right in the middle of the vows. Needless to say, the bride and groom got a substantial discount from the hotel, thanks to their contract. (Though that episode was so outrageous, perhaps that is the one case in which having a contingent contract wouldn't have been necessary!)

Date of Your Wedding

Then there's the question of when to get married. Let's say that you've found the location of your dreams. You must also think about when you'd like to get married and if the place will be available at that time. Let's assume that you are interested in a casual Sunday afternoon reception, and you ask the manager what daytime dates are available in June, only to hear that the site really works best at night-time. And, coincidentally, it turns out that the venue is available on Saturday nights for a bit more money.

Let's think about this for a moment. What the manager is trying to do is to get you to commit to another time when the site owners make more money. This is a form of entrapment. You may think you want a casual afternoon wedding, but some vendors may try to lead you toward a more glamorous and pricier night affair. Indeed, typically receptions on Saturday, at nearly any time of the day, are the most coveted and thus the most expensive. For some places the difference between a Friday and Saturday or between a Saturday and Sunday can be enormous. One luxury hotel in Philadelphia, for example, charges $35,000 more to get married on a Saturday than on a Friday.

Naturally, this can also be a form of bait and switch: A place will advertise that it offers the option of a less expensive Sunday reception but any date that you try to book is suspiciously unavailable. If you want the place, you'll have to go for a more expensive Saturday slot instead. In fact, when my friend Denise got married, she booked a Saturday night affair and was told that she was obligated to spend a certain amount of money on the reception in order to secure the room. When she realized that the total amount she planned to spend on food would not equal this amount, she was forced to spend additional funds, as the site would not refund the difference. And spend she did, adding a cappuccino machine, along with a host of fancy desserts. Of course the guests were happy, and often that's the most important goal, but it's hard to imagine that they would have been substantially less happy if Denise had been able to recoup some of the sizeable sum she ended up having to spend.

How to Handle It

With bait and switch, just being aware that it can happen can be your best protection. Of course, sometimes ignorance is bliss. Case in point: Betty, a school music teacher, went to a car dealer to buy a used car she had seen advertised in the newspaper. She did not realize that auto dealerships will often advertise a certain car knowing full well that there is only one such model on their entire lot and that most customers will have to pay more to get something comparable. Accordingly, she had dutifully gone to the bank beforehand and obtained a cashier's check for the entire amount she intended to spend. Faced with the possibility of losing a customer who was ready to pay in full for a car, the dealer backed down from his claim that the particular model she was interested in was only available for an additional fee. Herb Cohen, author of *You Can Negotiate Anything* (Bantam, 1982), offers similar advice: If there is a certain amount you are willing to spend and no more than that, write down the amount on a piece of paper ahead of time. That way, you will be less vulnerable to the pressures to overspend.

Did You Know?

When the officiate says "You may kiss the bride" this is meant to be more than just a token of affection. It has long been a custom and tradition that the kiss is a token of bonding as well as the exchange of spirits as each partner sends a part of themselves into the new spouse's soul, there to live ever after.

And by "spirits," we mean bacteria.

How Long Will Your Reception Last?

Consider not just the date of the location but how long you get to enjoy it. For example, my friend Gayle held her reception at a horticultural center. The location was booked until 11:30 p.m., but the catering staff, who were not affiliated with the site, wanted to leave at 10:30p.m. At around 10:15 that night, when the party was still in full swing, the caterers started to wrap up their service and take the tables and chairs with them. Granted they were willing to stay later—for a fee of $500 an hour! Gayle's parents had to turn their attention away from the celebration to consider their financial situation. Having already shelled out more than $20,000 to the caterer, they decided to end the reception early.

Another, more extreme version of this problem was featured on a recent segment on the ABC News/Primetime five-part series, *Weddings Gone Wild: Anything for Love* entitled "The Mug-Shot Bride." As chronicled on the show, the bride's family felt that the staff at the restaurant where the wedding took place tried to shut down the festivities early. For their part, the staff contended that the contracted time to use the bar had expired and that the people at the wedding were, in fact, raiding the bar. The young bride got very upset, argued with the staff, and allegedly hurled the wedding cake around. The owners called the police and the bride went to jail, affording amazing video of the bride in her wedding dress in a cell, spitting and cursing (lending credence to the idea that the bar should have been shut down even earlier!). In the end she was freed on a $1000 bond and later fined $90.

How to Handle It

1. Book a Place With Only 1 Wedding Per Day

Wherever you decide to hold your ceremony, make sure the place does not attempt to sandwich you in to an overbooked schedule. For example, some years ago Andrew and I attended the wedding of a mutual college friend. As we were leaving the church, the next wedding party was pacing around outside, leaving no time for a reception line or any other post-ceremony activities. As it happens, this was not a huge problem, as the groom had unfortunately fainted at the end of the ceremony and had been carted off to the hospital. Which leads me to my next piece of advice: If your future husband insists on a bachelor party, make sure it isn't the night before the wedding.

Because each bride wants to think that she's the only bride in the world, I recommend finding out whether you can book the place for the entire day. This means you can show up as early as you need to prepare for your day, and you can stay as late as you need to have fun. If you have your heart set on a place, either for your ceremony or your reception, that won't be yours exclusively, make sure there is enough time between weddings and, if possible, schedule your event to be the last of the day.

For example, the campus of Stanford University in Stanford, California features a fabulous church that is a favorite among engaged couples. Every weekend, the campus is teeming with brides and grooms, taking advantage of the spectacular location and balmy weather to hold their nuptials. Unless yours is the last wedding of the day, however, you can count on another wedding party filing in almost as soon as you have said I do. On the other hand, with a little advance planning, it may be possible to ensure that your wedding is the final one of the day, which means that you can probably count on finishing just as the sun is setting on the beautiful foothills surrounding the campus— and nobody cooling their heels while you're exchanging vows. Heck, even if you're not getting married, the church and the surrounding campus are worth a visit (there's my obligatory plug for my alma mater).

Of course, some places are so popular—and so large— that not only do they accommodate more than one wedding per day, they hold more than one wedding at the same time. Such an arrangement can work, as long as you confirm ahead of time (and note in your contract with the vendor) that there will be sufficient noise and crowd control—it's no fun having Hava Nagila blasting next door while you're trying to exchange solemn vows. Or worse, having uninvited drunk guests wander into your affair because they heard you have an open bar.

In short, if you want to get married at a popular location, consider this possibility carefully and consider how you would feel about other brides sharing the same space. Maybe you mind it and prefer to hold your wedding elsewhere. Maybe you're not too concerned. Maybe you can make provisions, agreeing to it, but only if the site includes separate wedding entrances. Learn what provisions the site has to guarantee your privacy and insist that those are included in your contract.

2. Do Not Rush Your Final Payment

It's best not to make your final payment to the reception site management until the end of your event. After all, once people have been paid in full for a job, there is less incentive for them subsequently to do their best for you. For example, I have been to several weddings in which the staff started to clean up too early; even before guests had had a chance to finish their dessert, it was whisked away. The result is that people get the sense that the party is over and begin to clear out. But if the staff is still waiting to receive a portion of their payment, they may be less apt to start cleaning up early and thus risk dissatisfying you. So be sure to inform the reception staff that you intend to complete payment at the end of your event.

Did You Know?

The tradition of tying old shoes to the car originated in England during the Tudor period. At that time, guests would throw shoes at the bride and groom as they left in their carriage. It was considered good luck if their carriage was hit. Today, more often than not, it is beverage cans that are tied to a couple's car instead of shoes. It should also be noted that the British consider it good luck if it rains on their wedding day!

Well, their shoes were probably already ruined by the rain, so what the heck.

Nibbling

So far we've discussed getting the right outdoor or indoor location, setting a good date for your day, and the optimal length of the reception. In addition to these basics, Patricia Lee, freelance writer and editor of WeddingeXpress (*weddingexpress.com*) recommends that you check out the following when visiting a reception site:

- Types of tables and chairs, table linen (choice of linen colors).
- Centerpieces/budvases available and cost.
- Reliable air conditioning.
- Dance floor large enough .
- Room and electrical accommodations for the DJ/ musicians.
- Restroom facilities adequate.
- Ample parking, valet service.
- Security provided.
- Room adequate for number of guests (not too large or small).

- 🌙 Adjoining rooms used by another party (if so, what is the noise level).
- 🌙 Make sure enough time has been allotted between reservations.
- 🌙 Make sure there is room for your gift table and cake table.

In addition, I caution you to be wary of any place that tries to nickel and dime you by adding a host of charges that you might have assumed would be covered by your initial fee, but (surprise, surprise) are not (what's often called nibbling). Indeed, if you are planning on taking a cruise for your honeymoon, you're likely to run across this same problem. Cruise lines lure you in by quoting a low price for the cruise itself and then failing to highlight the fact that almost everything is going to cost extra: soda and liquor, excursions to ports of call, photographs taken of your family, as well as, of course, the voluminous tips that you are expected to shell out for everyone from the maitre'd, headwaiter, and assistant waiter, to the housekeeping and room service staff. It all adds up—so much so that a "bargain" cruise can end up costing double what you thought it would.

How to Handle It

Try to consider, in advance, all the possible elements that you expect to be included in your ceremony and reception, and make sure they all appear in your contract. If there are additional elements that somehow escaped your attention and need to be included later, see if you can engage in trade-offs, or what are called gains of trade. For example, if you want to extend the reception and you also realize that you'll need valet service, see if the reception site proprietor will comp the extended time in exchange for your purchase of valet services. For more tips, see the chapter on catering.

Did You Know?

Traditionally, the bride had to enter her new home the first time through the front door. If she tripped or stumbled while entering, it was considered to be very bad luck. Hence the tradition of the groom carrying the bride over the threshold.

'Cuz everyone knows how much safer that is....

A Cautionary Note

When you visit a ceremony or reception site, sometimes the staff will offer you a list of recommended vendors (for example, a florist, caterer, photographer, or musician). Beware: Sometimes these are vendors who have paid to be on the list. In other words, you might want to take the various vendor recommendations offered by the site staff with a grain of salt. It may turn out that these are, in fact, the best providers for you, but all too often, they may instead be the best providers for the person recommending them to you.

Chapter Four

Catering

"Let's Give Them Something to Talk About..."

"Let's see...I'd like to start with smoked salmon coronets with herbed cream sauce along with the assortment of seasonal fresh fruits. Followed by a classical Caesar salad. Then I would like the roasted rack of lamb with herbs de Provence and Naturell Jus for the main course." Mmm... My mouth is watering with anticipation—is yours? Such is the kind of scrumptious, succulent tasting experience I hope your guests will have when eating your catered delights. Why? Plain and simple: One thing that everyone at a wedding seems to remember is the food. Consider the following snippet of conversation I overheard at a recent wedding:

> Guest 1: *"How's your chicken?"*
> Guest 2: *"It's overcooked. How's yours?"*

Now contrast it with another discussion (heard at a different wedding):

> Guest 1: *"How's your chicken?"*
> Guest 2: *"Delicious. It's perfectly cooked. Yours?"*

We all know which of these two conversations we'd prefer our guests to have. The challenge is to make sure your guests have the second conversation, not the first. After all, do you want your guests dining on something that makes cafeteria food look like haute cuisine? Or would you prefer they have a memorable experience eating the best wedding food they can remember—even without your having to fork over a bundle of cash to get it? If you choose the latter, this chapter is going to help you get there.

Once you have nailed down the date and time of your wedding, estimated the number of guests, and picked a ceremony and reception site, there's only one more major task: Find a groom. Just kidding. It's time to select the food. Of all the costs associated with your impending nuptials, the priciest will likely be the food. Unless you plan to hold a "peanut and pretzel" wedding, expect to pay more for food than for any other single aspect of your event. In addition to the actual food, typical catering charges can include beverages, kitchen staff, servers, equipment and tableware rentals, and decorations. Don't forget to add in the cost for renting the reception site itself and, on average, you're talking about 50 percent of your total wedding costs.

Of course some reception sites include all of the above and even throw in a Champagne toast and a cake. These "on-site locations" will typically quote you a flat rate for catering, bar service, table linens, and so on. This is what normally happens if you book a hotel, restaurant, or country club—places where there is one in-house caterer or banquet department and you meet with the reception manager to choose the type of foods and services you'd like.

At the opposite end of the spectrum, some places provide only the site itself. Known as "off-site locations," these include some reception halls, horticultural centers, or perhaps even your own summer beach house. (Don't we all wish we had one of those?) Because these sites typically offer few or none of the services you'll need, you'll want to hire one or more providers. In other words, you supply your own independent caterer (though they often give you a list of pre-approved caterers they use or recommend). Through your caterer you choose the food you'd like and identify what equipment the caterer will rent to you—which is practically everything. In fact, it's important to be very clear on that. A couple I know neglected to go over everything with the caterer and found out too late that the caterer did not intend to supply any plates. How he expected the guests to eat the food remains a mystery, but the couple was left scrambling to find a source for dishes at the 11th hour.

Location, Location, Location

Let's examine the pluses and minuses of each location option. On-site locations include most if not all of the amenities. As such, they often provide you with a rate that is either in terms of the number of guests (for example, $75 per guest) or one that represents the sum total that you will have to pay for the complete reception package. For example, the site I booked for my own wedding, a golf club in the suburbs of Philadelphia, gave me a quote of $15,000 for a Saturday event or $12,000 for a Sunday event (you'll recall from the ceremony chapter that non-Saturday dates are typically less popular but also typically cheaper. Supply and demand—it's true for the price of watermelons and it's true for reception sites). What would that price get you? Mine included "butlered hors d'oeuvres; first course, salad, entrée, and dessert; premium open bar for five hours; champagne or wine toast; wine service with dinner; all taxes and gratuities; valet parkers, coatroom attendant, and maid service." As for the food, I was presented with a menu of choices to spend my money on. There you have it—that's the typical on-site reception package. Easy as pie! (Or perhaps four-tiered, raspberry marzipan torte wedding cake—oh wait, that costs extra.)

Whereas an on-site location is typically all-inclusive, an off-site location requires you to start at the bottom and build your reception yourself, layer by layer, if you will. More specifically, you figure out everything you need and then take each element and multiply it by the number of guests you expect to invite. For instance, let's say you will be having 100 guests, and you want these guests to dine on steak. Suppose each steak dinner costs $40 per guest, amounting to a total of $4,000. Add to that $1000 for appetizers (say, for 3 appetizers), $1000 for drinks, and $500 for coffee/sodas. That's the food portion. But don't forget to figure in about $1,000 for rentals and $2500 for labor. That amounts to $10,000. Add the tax and gratuities, and your final tally is over $12,000, or over $120 per person.

Notice that in this example the total cost for the on-site versus off-site locations was essentially the same. But obviously that is not always the case. In general, expect to pay more at an on-site location. After all, you're paying for convenience: Everything is provided, so no need to shop around for various vendors. And you'll have fewer opportunities to negotiate, given that it can be more difficult to unpack an all-inclusive price into its constituent elements. (How can you negotiate the price of table rentals when you don't really know what portion of the total bill is devoted to such an item?)

By contrast, off-site locations will typically involve more work for you, given that you need to contract for everything you want at your reception, but you also have more of an opportunity to negotiate, as the cost of individual items is likely to be more apparent. If you are a seasoned negotiator or simply appreciate the opportunity to gain some bargaining experience, by all means feel free to negotiate. The best way to go about it is to research your preferences ahead of time and solicit bids from different places.

For example, say you'd like to have chicken at your reception. Shop around and you'll find plenty of caterers willing to accommodate you, though it's best to have a more specific idea of what you want (for example, chicken with a pesto sauce) to make comparison shopping easier (otherwise you could end up comparing apples to oranges, as in apple glazed chicken to chicken l'orange). Build up your menu as a complete package (including linens, servers, drink service, and so on) so that the quotes you obtain will be for the total catering price. (And don't forget plates!)

Once you have collected your quotes, set an upper bound, that is, the most you'd be willing to spend, and a target price, the smaller amount that you'd actually prefer to spend. Your major strategy is to play the caterers off each other. For example, you might say to one caterer:

> *"Another caterer quoted me a price of*
> *$20 less a head—can you beat it?"*

If yes, than go back to first vendor and ask him or her to beat the newer, lower price. Keep going until one vendor says he or she can't offer a better deal. In this way, you should be able to receive lower and lower bids, allowing you to close in on your target price.

At this point you still have options: You can book the caterer who has just offered you the best deal, or, if you are feeling adventurous and want to try for more, you can nibble for a little extra. For instance, try saying,

> *"I agree to that price, but I would appreciate it if you*
> *could add one more food station/side dish/appetizer [feel free*
> *to fill in with your own desired option]."*

This is also called nibbling, the addition of a new request after tentative agreement has already been reached but before the deal is officially sealed. If the caterer agrees, you just got a smidgeon more for your money. If they don't agree, don't give up yet. Instead, you can try the following:

"Okay, if you can't do X, what can you do?"

It doesn't hurt to ask, and you might just win a further concession. In fact, if the caterer does offer something extra, be prepared to sign the contract—given that you pressed the other side and got something in return, you should be willing to close the deal. If the caterer still doesn't budge, you have two choices: Sign anyway, knowing that you tried your hardest (contrary to popular mythology, *not* everything is negotiable), or wait a day or two before agreeing to the caterer's terms—terms that may become more favorable during the interim.

In negotiating with a caterer (or any service provider, for that matter), you may be forced to press the other side a little. That's fine if you feel uncomfortable with that notion. Just remember to be professional and diplomatic. Feel free to say something such as:

"I don't mean to be a bother, but this wedding is a big expense for me and I need to get the best price possible. [This other caterer] can offer this price. Can you meet it?"

Notice there's even a hint of an apology in there—anything to cushion your request and ensure that you seem reasonable.

Whether you choose an on-site location or an off-site location, expect wide variation across the country in what you can expect to pay. According to one source, the nationwide average price for wedding reception catering, including food, beverages, equipment rentals, labor costs, and gratuities is a little more than $50 a person. This average can run as high as

$150 a person in big cities (like where I planned my own wedding, Philadelphia). Some caterers charge as much as $200 per guest, and I've even heard of higher rates, and I bet you have too.

Hors D'oeuvres, Anyone?

As I've mentioned, you will be spending a large proportion of your budget on catering. But before you do so, you get a little treat that may lift your spirits: the food tasting. In between your initial consultation with caterers and actually booking one of them, brides and their families typically arrange a time to sample the caterer's cuisine. This tasting often takes place at the caterer's establishment.

I view the tasting session as a dress rehearsal for the food as well as for the caterer. As you sample the food, obviously you want to make observations about how well the food is cooked, how tasty is it, and how nicely it's presented. But I advise you to go beyond the food to study the demeanor of the server. Note whether particular caterers are positive, helpful, and knowledgeable. Feel free to ask them how a certain item was prepared and listen to their responses. You can see if they offer anything complimentary—an extra hors d'oeuvre, a second slice of the dessert cake, or a glass of wine. You can even request something gratis and note their response. Finally, check out the serving wear, napkins, and tablecloths.

How Much Should I Order?

As I'm suggesting, if the caterers are good, they should do their utmost to ensure you have a good time sampling their food. Clearly it's in their interest to have you book your wedding with them. But they may also be pursuing a subtler goal, of which you should also be aware. While you sample the food, they may try to get you to spend a lot more on catering than perhaps you had originally intended. In other words, when caterers throw in those seemingly free additional samples here and there, remember that, just as there's no such thing as a free lunch, there's not usually a free sampling menu. Yes, it's possible they're just being kind, but it's equally possible that they're trying to tempt you to return the favor by ordering pricier entrées or additional items, whether they be appetizers, side dishes, or desserts. Reciprocity is a powerful force—even when someone gives you something you didn't ask for, you can feel compelled to give that person something in return.

How to Handle It

Like so many negotiations, a great way to handle this form of entrapment is to be prepared. Before you begin to sample any food, ask for the pricing in advance. Indeed, have the price list in front of you while you try everything; that way you can see immediately how much extra it will cost to add that tiny little, seemingly innocuous, appetizer (for example "foie gras," which should be French for "large bill"). If you need to, feel free to say,

"I would be grateful for a list of menu offerings and prices as I sample the foods. It would really help me to have the package list at my side."

Okay, so hopefully by now you've sampled some good food, ideally while keeping track of the costs (best not to drink too much wine, lest those calculations become unwieldy). Now it's the end of the night and you are ready to leave. Do you have to pay the caterer for the tasting? Well, depending on the caterer, some will offer you a free tasting but others may charge a price—some a rather hefty fee of $100 (incidentally, if a caterer does not provide any sort of tasting opportunity, I'd recommend selecting a different caterer). What about those caterers who want to charge you for a tasting? This amount may be more negotiable than you think. For example, first you can try to get the caterer to waive the fee:

"I'm going to be spending a substantial amount (or insert amount in the thousands) of money on your catering. So, if you could comp this tasting, I would very much appreciate it."

If you are willing to do a little advanced planning, some experts recommend that you suggest having your tasting coincide with another meal that the caterer is already preparing, necessitating only the preparation of a couple extra plates. Still another way is to ask for a complimentary, though limited menu (for example, a free dinner for two as opposed to four, or one that includes just three appetizers rather than six). In essence, if you have a pretty good idea of what kind of food you want, you can try to limit yourself to just those selections, as opposed to trying a little of everything.

If the caterer does not agree to provide you with a complimentary full meal or even a mini meal, I would, at the very least, insist on a discount. For example, you can mention that you agree to pay for the food costs only. My husband, who was trained as a chef, tells me that for successful caterers, the cost of the food is only 1/3 of the total retail price of the meal. Which means that, at least when it comes to your little sampling experience, approximately 2/3 of the bill is profit. So there is some flexibility there for the caterer to come down in price.

And then there was cake.

Grains have long symbolized fertility. During ancient times, wedding ceremonies were finalized by breaking a large loaf of bread above the head of the bride. After the loaf was broken, the wedding guests would gather the crumbs as tokens of good luck. Eventually, the bread was replaced by cakes, which became more elaborate over the centuries.

Entrapment

Earlier I mentioned the idea of entrapment during the sample tasting. Caterers may try to entice you not just to go with their services but to order additional food—and more expensive food at that. Now let's discuss additional ways that caterers may try to entrap you to spend more, beginning with the very first meeting.

When they first meet you, caterers will typically try to get a sense of your preferences (for example, sit-down meal versus buffet) and how much you're willing to spend. For my wedding, I envisioned my reception including some appetizers during the cocktail hour followed by a sit-down meal including salad, a main course, dessert, and wedding cake. That struck me as a fairly standard request.

Unfortunately, even though we may have a basic idea of what we want in our heads, once we meet with caterers it's easy to get carried away. For example, if you want a reception featuring food stations, caterers may try to lure you into choosing additional food stations, so that two stations (meat and side dishes) suddenly becomes four, including exotic stations (for example, crepe station, kids station) or fancier food options. You may even be tempted to add options that you never previously imagined. ("A cappuccino section would just happen to fit so nicely in the corner area over here...") This is entrapment: The longer you stay in the situation, the more you are tempted to overspend.

How does this entrapment happen? Sometimes it simply emerges out of an innocent-seeming conversation with a caterer, as he or she describes all the wonderful foods you "simply must have at your wedding." The longer you meet with the caterer, the more you may begin to consider options that you never even knew you wanted and then, voila you've just got to have those red grapes with gorgonzola cheese and walnuts.

But it doesn't stop there—I recall situations in which a caterer would tempt and tease me with all these elaborate catering concepts but fail to quote prices for any of it. And I'm not alone. For my friend Lori, one caterer prepared an elaborate menu based on their earlier discussions but somehow the prices were oh-so-conveniently omitted. Beware: This is often no accident! Caterers often "forget" to include prices in the sample menu because they want you to fall in love with all the wonderful food options before you are forced to swallow the bitter pill known as the bill. Of course, caterers aren't alone in this. It seems to me that the fancier the restaurant, the less likely they are to tell you how much anything costs. I think there ought to be a law that says restaurants have to tell you up front how much everything costs, and if you have to ask, your meal is free. Who's with me? Let's start a petition drive!

Anyway, consider the following two food options for a wedding reception taken from an actual menu:

Roast Sliced Loin of Pork filled with herbed
Apple-Walnut stuffing
Served with Cognac Carbonade

Fresh Breast of Chicken wrapped
in Crisp Feuille De Brik
With a rich filling of Fresh Leek and Mushrooms

Yum, yum! This sounds delicious and I don't even understand all the words! Carbonade? That sounds like some sports drink ("replenishes all the carbon your body loses as you sweat"). And I assume that Feuille De Brik doesn't

actually refer to the stuff they put between building blocks
to hold up a wall ("Say, Larry, you better Feuille De Brik
before the whole structure comes tumbling down!"). But
perhaps it won't sound quite so appetizing if we try it again,
this time with some added numbers:

Roast Sliced Loin of Pork filled
with herbed Apple-Walnut stuffing
Served with Cognac Carbonade
$80

Fresh Breast of Chicken wrapped
in Crisp Feuille De Brik
With a rich filling of Fresh Leek and Mushrooms
$75

Apparently, it costs a lot to add those fancy words! You
see how it's harder to get swept away when you have those
numbers there to ground you. Caterers know they will eventually have to confront you with prices, but, like the less-
than-honest suitor who tells you he's a prince when he's
actually a pauper, they want to delay that reality until you've
already fallen in love with the product.

On other occasions, caterers will give you a quote that
includes services you didn't ask for. Here they may be
counting on that age-old adage: "It's easier to get forgive-
ness than permission." The idea is that you are less likely
to ask for a particular charge to be removed from a bill
once it already appears there. A friend of mine recently got
married. When she asked a caterer for a quote, it included
a host of extras she didn't want, and, not surprisingly, the
total ended up being much higher than she had anticipated.
Clearly, the caterer was relying on the assumption that in
the midst of all the wedding preparations, we may be reluctant to take the time to haggle. But haggle you should.

How to Handle It

1. First, Ask for Pricing!

When the caterer suggests a new item, ask how much it will cost or, if you prefer subtlety:

"How much will that add to the total bill?"

2. Know Your Limits

Keep your budget in mind and don't go over it. Decide in advance what percentage of your total wedding budget you plan to devote to catering, and stick to that limit. And be aware that caterers typically prepare food for a few extra guests without being asked. One of Andrew's relatives learned this fact a little too late, and ended up paying for meals for a number of guests who didn't show up to her daughter's wedding. She later realized that she could have simply told the caterer (and paid for!) a number that was slightly smaller than the number of invited guests and still had enough food for everyone.

3. Think Like a Caterer

My husband (who, you'll recall, went to culinary school—lucky me!) suggests that another way to maintain a realistic budget is to put yourself in the shoes of the caterer. According to this mindset, there are two basic sources of costs to a caterer: the cost of the food itself and the cost of the labor to prepare and serve the food.

Let's imagine that you are considering offering your wedding guests a choice of grilled chicken fillet or grilled steak at your wedding. When comparing the two, from a caterer's perspective, the cost of food may be a few dollars higher for the steak (picture yourself shopping for each at the supermarket). The cost of labor, however, is essentially the same: you're doing the same preparation for the chicken or the beef: putting meat on the grill and cooking it until it's done.

With this in mind, you can deduce that the steak should cost only slightly more than the chicken. So if the caterer charges 50 percent more for the steak, you know that the price is not really justified. Consequently, you can bargain harder to keep the price down. In other words, if the caterer suggests upgrading from chicken to steak, don't automatically agree to a higher price. Request a comparable price or one that is only slightly higher. Alternatively, ask the caterer to throw in something else. For example, "I'll pay more for the steak, but I'd like an additional side dish as well."

4. Ask for the Blue Plate Special

Although I don't know the derivation of the term (did restaurants really serve bargain meals on blue plates?), don't hesitate to press the caterer for additional discounts, perhaps starting with the removal of extras that you don't need. This is what my friend Lori did, telling the caterers during successive discussions to take off items and readjust the price. Try saying something such as,

> *"The menu seems to include items that I did not request. Can you take them off and readjust the price?"*

I know it may make you a bit uncomfortable to say something, but you shouldn't have to pay for items you don't want. After all, you're not buying a luxury automobile.

A Matter of Choice

As long as we're talking about adding more and more options to the table, there is one final matter I'd like to mention. Besides the issue of just how much food to order, there is the question of choice. Much like Shakespeare's "To be or not to be," a fundamental question in life, at least when it comes to wedding receptions, is: A choice of main entrées or not? Okay, your dilemma might not be as dire as Hamlet's was, but unless you offer a buffet or food stations, you might wrestle with whether you should provide one dish for all guests, or have guests choose between two dishes.

Personally, I like the idea of a choice, but beware of caterers who claim to be offering choice but in reality surreptitiously limit guests to one option. For example, one caterer my friend Lori came across tried to present her with the illusion of choice. He asked Lori to choose whether she preferred fish for every guest, or beef instead. The caterer then explained that once each table was served, the wait staff would come around with a handful of the alternate dish and inquire if any of the guests (with their plates already in front of them, mind you) would like their food "choice" changed. At that point it's a little late; most guests would probably feel that switching dinner plates would be, at the very least, awkward, and it could very well be the case that guests have already started eating. In essence, the clever caterer was pretending to offer two main dish options, and planning to charge Lori as such, but really only offering one. No, I don't think so.

Pricey Extras

When it comes to hiring a caterer, food isn't the only issue. There are other incidental charges that may fill up your plate. I've already mentioned how caterers may attempt to charge you for the tasting session. And in the next chapter I'll help you tackle caterers (well, not literally) who try to charge you for serving and cutting your wedding cake. Aside from these, there may be a corkage fee if you supply your own wine; a premium for bartending services; a cost for chairs; a surcharge for appliances such as a stove, refrigerator, or outdoor heaters; charges for plates, cookware, servingware, flatware, stemware, foodware. (Okay, I made up that last one, but I wouldn't be surprised to see it on a catering bill.)

You get my drift—there are lots of potential additional charges to pad your bill.

To be sure, some of these charges may be reasonable and you should expect to pay for these services/products. Particularly for off-site locations where you have to contract out for service and equipment, you must accept that you will have to pay for some equipment and for servers.

But sometimes charges can get a bit excessive. As I'm writing this, I am thinking of a caterer's proposal that is beside me, which itemizes separate prices for tables of various lengths and shapes; assorted drinking-wear (glasses, goblets, and mugs); and plates of all sizes. There is no reason for you to pay a charge for driving time (I've seen it for $7 an hour). Nor should you pay a clean-up fee (Yes, I've seen that too!)—after all, isn't that the caterer's job?

How to Handle It

1. Just Say No

If you are faced with an inflated charge, the first thing to do is just to refuse to pay it. Be positive but firm. Let's say that you are told that there is an additional fee for the servers to come in proper dress. How should you respond?

> A) "Could you take this charge off? If you can't, that's okay."
>
> B) "Could you take this charge off?"
>
> C) "Could you take this charge off because I think a fair price does not have to involve an additional fee for attire?"
>
> D) "Could you take this charge off because I would like it removed?"

What's the correct answer? Well, certainly not Option A, which is too wishy-washy: Adding that second sentence gives the caterer a way out. Actually, *any* of the other choices would be correct. You can simply ask for the charge to be removed and wait patiently, letting the other party sweat a little and feel motivated to respond. Or, if you prefer, you can give a reason—a legitimate one as in Option C or even a placebo-like one as in Option D. Sometimes you don't need a real reason—just phrasing your request in a format that seems to suggest a legitimate reason can be sufficient to get a positive response.

2. Ask for Justification

If refusing to pay doesn't work or is not your cup of tea, you can ask for the rationale behind an inflated charge. Can the caterer easily defend or justify the charge, or does he or she squirm while hemming and hawing? For example, some caterers add an 18 percent service charge that is anything but clearly defined. What is it? And how is it different from taxes and gratuities that may already be included on a bill? When asked, the caterer may explain that it is a customary charge that covers one meeting, décor, and tasting. Let's break that down: you are paying money to meet with the caterer? That's silly; the consultation should be free. I don't know what falls under décor (because the food is plenty of decoration already). Which leaves you with what appears to be a disguised charge for the food tasting. In sum, just asking the caterer to spell out exactly what a charge is for may pressure him or her to reduce or eliminate it. And all you're doing is asking—what could be easier than that?

3. Know Your Options

As I've said over and over again, when it comes to negotiating, it's a truism that preparation is key. In this case, if every caterer you've researched includes the same questionable charge on the bill, it may not be negotiable. But if you encounter some caterers who don't, you can assume it is not standard procedure, and most likely the charge can be waived. For example, one catering company that I came across in my research boasted that they do not add gratuities, cake-cutting fees, or corkage fees. If they don't, why should anyone? Likewise don't be suckered into the idea of paying an hourly rate for each server used. Some caterers will try to get away with as much as $25 per hour per server; at that point it's time to find another caterer.

Nibbling

When it comes to catering, nibbling is a bad thing—not the kind that might cause your waistline to expand, but the kind that causes your wallet to shrink. As we've seen elsewhere, in a negotiation, nibbling refers to last minute requests that occur near the end of a bargaining session, when you're tired and thus more apt to agree to something unreasonable while getting nothing in return. To be sure, sometimes the nibble is a small bite (and maybe you want to agree to it). But other times the nibble can be larger, taking a substantial chunk out your budget.

How to Handle It

The best way to guard against nibbling is to assemble all your requests for your caterer ahead of time—everything from drink requests to serving needs to menu preferences. If you have a predetermined list of all your needs, when you meet with a caterer, you can preempt the infliction of additional last-minute charges. Another advantage of knowing what you need ahead of time is that you can take advantage of bulk purchasing. Think of it like buying items A + B + C + D as being cheaper than buying A + B + C, and adding D later on. You get a lower price for the former because merchants prefer larger orders and are willing to offer discounts to get them. But if you ask for items individually, merchants are likely to try to maximize profit on each, and end up charging you more than if you had asked for all the items at once.

Add Your Own Nibble

Recognize that many brides don't end up eating at their own reception—they're too busy, stressed, excited, or maybe all of the above. After all that preparation and planning, it seems a shame not to even get to taste the food you so lovingly selected. The solution? Crash another wedding put on by your same caterer. Just kidding. Alternatively, ask the caterer to box up your food or, better yet, ask to have a couple of additional meals prepared and packed up for consumption later. As we said before, most caterers prepare extra meals anyway—you might as well enjoy the fruits of their labor—and yours.

Bait and Switch

Once you've envisioned the kind of food you'd like to be served at your wedding, tasted the sample catering delights, and placed your order, you want to feel sure that the catering service on the day of your wedding will be of the same quality. The best way to ensure this is to have the same catering representative you've been meeting with be present on your wedding day. Otherwise, if the caterers substitute a different manager, for example, that person may not be as familiar with your account and not do things to your liking. Indeed, before your big day, some experts recommend observing another wedding reception put on by your caterer to ensure the service is up to par. Mind you, I didn't say "crash," I said "observe."

How to Handle It

Another way to prevent being the victim of bait and switch is to confirm in advance that the person handling your account will be present throughout your wedding. If that person will not be present, find out who will and make sure you are comfortable working with that individual—after all, he or she will be your contact if anything goes awry on the day in question. Don't forget to note the name of the contact person in the contract so that the caterer is under some obligation to show up or face a financial penalty.

Contract Fundamentals

Speaking of the contract, here's a list of essentials to include in yours:

- The wedding date and location, and the time and hours of service that the caterer will be providing.
- The services provided (sit-down meal, bar service, wedding cake, and so on).
- The itemized menu (including provisions for special meals).
- Timeline of the wedding (what order is the meal served, as well as the when and where).
- Date you need to provide the final head count to the caterer.
- The fees (and extra expenses); schedule of payment (including date final balance is due); Some caterers will ask for the complete payment in advance of the day, some ask for it on the wedding day, and I've even heard of the balance being due two to three days afterward. Insist on one of the two latter options. Otherwise, if you pay in advance, you have much less recourse if something doesn't go as it should.
- The caterer's cancellation policy.
- The name of the caterer and his or her contract information.

Finally, the contract should also include any special details that are unique to your wedding. For example, you can ask that a fruit dish be served fresh, not pre-set on the table ahead of time, in order to preserve its flavor. Or maybe you want the curtains in the reception hall to be opened during the meal. I also encourage you to include a clause stating that no bussing of drinks or desserts will occur until the end of the reception. Likewise, I wrote in my contract that creams, sugars, and coffee should be left on the tables throughout the evening even if guests leave. My goal in voicing these requests was to ensure that my guests would not feel like they were being rushed out the door before the festivities had even come to a close. Plus I wanted to placate Andrew, who is still bitter about a wedding reception he attended years ago in which the serving staff removed his dessert while he had gotten up to dance. "But that chocolate mousse looked really good, Shirit!" "Time to let it go, Andrew."

All righty then—Bon Appetit!

Chapter Five

Cake

To many, a wedding without a cake is like Christmas without a tree—it just isn't a celebration. But wedding cakes are expensive—just ask Steve Martin's character in the remake of *Father of the Bride,* which, coincidentally, was playing on TV the day I was working on this chapter. When he learns that the cake is going to cost $1,200, he exclaims that his first car didn't cost that much. Actually the average cost of a wedding cake for 175 guests is more than $500: a hefty sum, to be sure—maybe that's why the tradition arose for the bride and groom to save their leftover cake for the first year of their marriage—at those prices, best not to waste any.

When selecting a cake there's a lot to consider: there's the size and shape of the cake; the layers of filling, like chocolate versus fruit (which often means his favorite filling versus hers); and of course the decorations (which often means those corny figures on the top or not). In addition to these choices, there's another decision that you'll want to make early in your cake pursuit. That is, where will you get your cake? Should you purchase it from the caterer who's planning to do your reception or should you go with an independent baker?

Suppose, for example, that there is a neighborhood bakery that you have frequented for years. Given that you like the selection and have a relationship with the baker, you might assume that this is the best place to order your cake. But hold on just a moment. Before you arrange to go with your favorite baker, find out if the caterer or reception hall is going to charge you extra to bring in a cake from somewhere else. In fact, at many establishments you can expect to pay about $1 per slice for the privilege of *not* using the in-house pastry chef. That's right: You may have to pay a premium to have the cake of your dreams.

So before you do anything else, first check whether there is such a charge in your reception hall or catering contract. And then relax. In this chapter I'll show you how to negotiate to avert this and other challenges—after all, the rationale, or the "principle," to use negotiation terms, behind such a charge is not always defensible (does it really cost more to cut and serve a cake that happened to be baked somewhere else?), and the other side may back down.

Whether or not you choose to go with the on-site provider for your cake, I suggest that, at the minimum, you discuss the issue with the baker or caterer the site typically uses as they may be a good source to help you figure out what kind of cake you want. Feel free to bring along pictures you've torn out of magazines, drawings, samples of wedding colors, and any other ideas you have. And don't forget to sample cakes. I know...poor you! By the way, as you taste, notice how generous and friendly the staff is. When a friend of mine was investigating reception sites, the on-site caterer was more than generous when it came to providing sample dinner fare. However, when it came time to sample a cake, my friend barely got a chance to try a bite before the rest of the slice was whisked away, never to return—were they hiding something? I maintain that if the catering staff doesn't seem like they want to work with you, I wouldn't encourage you to negotiate with them. It's not worth the hassle. There's another baker out there who really wants your business and will show it.

> *It's probably not a good sign if one of them decides to delegate the task to the other.*
>
> Cutting the cake symbolizes the first task a couple handles together once married.

Entrapment

As with the rest of your catering options, entrapment can all too easily occur when you are selecting a cake. How so? Well, one ploy is to tempt you with what are called "couture-esque" cakes—designer cakes with fancy extras like a photo of the bride and groom or decorated with imprints of the gown or the couple's initials. In general, unless you're Carmen Electra, who reportedly had a cake that was decorated with $700 worth of Swarovski crystals, my advice is best not to succumb to the temptation—after all, you *are* planning to eat the thing!

Bait and Switch

In addition to the pressure to order fancy cake accessories, there are several other devious tactics to look out for when ordering a cake, many of which come under the heading of bait and switch: You think you're getting one thing, only to learn some time later that you're getting something else—something else less desirable. Here are three versions to watch out for:

What's My Size?

Imagine that you're in a grocery store looking for healthy food, and you check a label on a particular product and are initially thrilled to see how few calories there are in a serving—only to discover that a serving is smaller than your last breath mint. Unfortunately, this same kind of misleading information can crop up when you are trying to order a wedding cake. Say you ask your cake makers for an estimate of the price. What you may very well get is an estimate per slice. Only later do you learn that their estimate was for a very thin two-inch slice, while you were hoping for a more realistic four-inch slice. So be sure to ask each baker you're considering what the size of a slice is.

Where's My Baker?

Sometimes you may contract with one cake designer only to learn that someone else will be delivering and setting up your cake on your special day. This may be fine, unless your cake requires some expert last-minute assistance. (Nobody likes a droopy cake!) So it might behoove you to ascertain and indicate on your contract the name of the person who will actually be delivering the cake and what happens if there is a problem on the day itself.

Lookin' Good!

When a baker shows you photos of cakes, make sure they're photos of real cakes actually produced by that individual or staff. Some bakeries use standard cake-design books and tell brides they can design anything found in these publications. But when they attempt to pull off one of those designs, the results can be disappointing. So, when considering a particular baker, check out the cakes in the store, look at pictures of cakes actually produced by that establishment, and/ or attend cake tastings sponsored by that baker.

Tastin' Good!

Which brings me to my next point: the taste test. Let's say you've been able to determine that yes, the baker you're interested in really does produce pretty cakes. That's great, but what about the taste? Pretty cakes may not all taste good. So taste-test the cake. Make sure the cake is not too dry. Find that right amount of moisture that makes your mouth water. Unless you just want to look at your cake, the inside is just as important as the outside. Incidentally, taste sampling should not cost you money. If a baker wants to charge you, I recommend that you find another; but if you have your heart set on this particular individual, try some negotiation techniques, such as:

1. Liking

The nicer you are to the vendor the more likely you'll get results. So smile as you look around. Make some small talk. Then ask directly for a free tasting but in a sweet tone so as to encourage liking, such as: "I heard you offer samples, yes?" If necessary add the following:

"Only for a price? Darn. We would really like to order a cake from you but we just want to make sure we like the flavor."

If the baker agrees to this small request, he or she is more likely to be flexible later on when it comes time to negotiate the terms of your order.

2. Contingent Contract

You're trying to woo the salesperson with flattery, but what if the baker still wants to charge you something for samples? If you think about it, what he or she really wants is the big bucks when you order a cake. As for you, you are willing to pay those big bucks but you want to shave off the cost of sampling. The uncertainty here involves whether or not you will actually order the cake. So you have the advantage. Try suggesting to the baker that you'll pay for the tasting, but should you decide to order a cake, the cost will be deducted from the final bill. Such a gesture is likely to motivate the baker to do a good job for you, as it signals your desire for further business dealings, even as it could save you money in the long run.

3. Last Resort

If all else fails, and you really don't want to pay for samples, as I alluded to previously, you can try attending a cake tasting that bakers occasionally offer.

"Let Them Eat Cake (For an Additional Fee)": Nibbling

Normally, when it comes to cakes, a little nibbling is a good thing. But in this case, I'm not talking about stealing a bit of frosting from an unseen corner—I'm talking about those little extra concessions that the other side tries to win from you in a negotiation, right before the deal is closed. I already mentioned the additional charge for cake-tasting that the baker or caterer may try to inflict. Here are some additional examples of what to avoid:

1. Mixing Flavors?

Let's say you and your intended like different kinds of cake—maybe you like vanilla, as I do, but your fiancé likes chocolate, as my co-author does. What are you to do? Why, call off the wedding of course! No! Actually, why not get both? Many bakeries will accommodate your desire to have two or even more flavors in a cake, typically in separate tiers, but some will want to charge extra for this "premium" service. If that happens, how should you handle it?

For starters, don't be afraid to ask bakers what justifies the higher price for a different flavor. Flavoring itself costs next to nothing. In fact, if they are using extract (a concentrated artificial flavor that most bakeries use) to flavor the cake, there is no difference in cost whether you are getting one or a dozen different flavors: whether the baker puts in a teaspoon of vanilla extract or a teaspoon of almond extract—it costs the same. Now if there are real ingredients in the cake, such as actual almonds or Belgian chocolate, then understandably having different flavors will cost a little more. But be sure to check this out: Ask them if they are adding actual ingredients or just flavoring. If the latter, no need to pay more.

2. How About a Few Extras?

In addition to charging you for added flavors, the baker may want to charge you for delivery and/or the rental of certain accessories. These rentals may include cake toppers; cake cutters; cake stands; flowers, either real or silk; and even complex decorations such as ornamental fountains. When considering such extras, I recommend that you first figure out what you want in advance to determine whether you will be charged separately for each addition. The more preparation you do in advance, the more you avoid last-minute surprises. In general, when it comes to cake accessories, I think less is more. You want your cake to stand on its own. So remember to carefully consider which extras you really want and which you can do without. (Who wants a fountain near a cake anyway?)

3. The Dreaded Cake-Cutting Fee

As with the extra costs associated with catering, some additions to your cake, such as flowers, you should naturally be charged for, but others may be inappropriate. For example, it's typical for the cake maker to charge you for delivering the cake, but the reception site may also charge you to cut the cake, and this charge may be described as just a slight additional fee, say $1 per person, which doesn't sound like much till you add it all up (it's like those commercials that tell you that for just "pennies a day" you can have some high-priced item that you don't really need or want). Wedding reception sites often charge this fee to discourage you from using outside bakers. Some wedding sites will try to charge you the cake-cutting fee regardless of whether you use an in-house baker or not. And they may even try to charge you for cake-cutting knives, at which point you may feel like you need a knife, but not for cutting the cake.

How to Handle It

1. Refuse

As simple as it sounds, one strategy is simply to refuse to pay it—nicely, of course. Say something such as,

> "Yes, I was really hoping to avoid any additional charges, in light of the overall cost of the event."

Then pause—the ball will then be in their court. It's amazing how effective simply pausing can be—people often feel obligated to fill empty conversation space, especially during tense moments—let the other side fill it, ideally with an offer to remove the charge. If no offer is forthcoming, then you can try the more direct approach with a polite query such as, "Can you waive that charge for me?"

2. Ask Them to Reciprocate

Let's say the other side still won't budge. No need to give up yet. You can try insisting on reciprocal concessions. In other words, you can agree to pay the fee but get something for yourself in the deal. Try saying something such as:

"All right, I am willing to pay the cake-cutting fee, but I'd like to make sure the cake is served only at the proper time and the leftovers are promptly boxed for us and our guests to take home."

After all, if you are going to make a concession and pay the egregious fee, you should be entitled to a concession in return.

The Groom's Cake

The tradition of a "Groom's Cake" comes from England and Ireland. There, the traditional groom's cake is a fruitcake with white icing. The groom's cake is usually served along with the traditional wedding cake. Today groom's cakes are very often chocolate instead of the traditional fruitcake.

By this point in history, that traditional fruitcake has probably gotten pretty stale.

Timing

Unlike other aspects of your wedding, when it comes to ordering a cake, you can get away with doing this one within two months of your date—even less with some commercial bakeries, a little more if you're the anxious type. The real trick is to make sure you coordinate the timing of the delivery of the cake. You don't want a cake that is dropped off too early and left unattended. Ideally, the cake should be delivered not more than two hours before the reception and left in the capable hands of someone at the reception site. If you're concerned, inquire about guarantees from the baker—you should be entitled to a reduction in price if your terms are not met. And remember to find out how late you can update your final guest total to ensure the proper size cake arrives on your magical day.

Contract Fundamentals

Here are some items that you want to include in your cake contract:

- Cake design (and shape).
- Flavors.
- Filling.
- Color.
- Cake topper.
- Other decorations.
- Number (of guests) to serve.
- Rentals (for example, a table to hold the cake, cake stand).
- Delivery (and set-up?) charge.
- Delivery time and place.
- Approximate cost per slice.
- Tax.
- Deposit.
- Total.

With all of these items accounted for, you can feel free to, as they say, have your cake and eat it too (though I'm not sure what else you'd do with a cake).

Chapter Six

Music

I've had the time of my life
And I never felt this way before
Yes I swear—it's the truth
And I owe it all to you!

I t's hard not to sing along, isn't it? Remember that little ditty from *Dirty Dancing*? I'm a little embarrassed to admit it, but it's one of my favorite songs. So when it came time for my wedding, I insisted on it. In fact, it closed our wedding reception because I wanted my guests to feel like they had the time of their lives at my wedding. And, of course, I want you to have the best time at yours!

So how do we accomplish that? One word: music. Music is the glue that holds your wedding together. It's the classical music to which you might march down the aisle. It's the often jazzy but typically not-too-loud music you use for your cocktail hour to let guests mingle or during dinner while they're eating. It's that sentimental song that gets your guests teary eyed when you do the father-daughter dance. And it's that upbeat mix that gets your guests to the dance floor, even Cousin Edie, bless her heart: six weeks post hip replacement and she can't help herself—now that's a sign of good music (or poor medical judgment)!

Because music is one key to your day, make it high on your priority list and don't wait until it's too late to book the kind of music you really want. In fact, some sources warn that popular wedding bands can be booked up if you call them less than a year in advance. (And you thought booking a spouse was the challenging part.)

Any discussion about music at the reception will inevitably come down to the age-old question: Does anybody actually like accordion music? Sorry, the question I meant was, Should you choose a DJ or a band? Let me tip my hand right away: How much do you want to spend? Obviously, a band will typically cost more than a DJ because you are paying for more than one person, plus their instruments, of course. But there is also a large range in prices, with factors such as the popularity of the band, time of year, day of the week, and duration of the event all potentially affecting how much you will have to pay. According to experts, the average price for a four-piece band for four hours on a Saturday can range from $500 to $5000; for DJs, it's $400 to $1200. In big cities, prices obviously run toward the upper end of the scale, if not past it, depending on your package. As you can see, there is overlap in the two price scales, meaning that sometimes you'll find an expensive DJ that costs more than some bands. In other words, what this boils down to is that while a band is generally pricier than a DJ, there are expensive DJs, as well as inexpensive bands.

At least it's not, "What's Love Got to Do With It."

The most popular first dance song is
"What a Wonderful World" by Louis Armstrong.

Okay, so this matter isn't so easily resolved. Given that there is some price overlapping here, I suggest that you not only consider the finances but also the style of wedding you'd like to have. Let's discuss the feel of a DJ versus a band. Try picturing a DJ: an energetic MC spinning your favorite tunes and engaging in playful banter with the guests. Now try visualizing a band—a rousing rock trio or perhaps a stately string quartet or a regal brass quintet. In some ways, it depends not only on the kind of music you like, but also on the formality of the event itself, the feel of the place in which you plan to hold your wedding and/or reception, and even the time of day. A heavy-metal band, no matter how rousing, probably won't work at an afternoon ceremony in an English-style country garden (even if the band members do have the right accent). Whichever way you end up going, I'm here to help. I can't play an instrument or sing (although, let me tell ya, Andrew does a mean Ave Maria), but I can help you negotiate the price down for whichever option you choose.

One additional piece of advice: If you are getting married in a church or synagogue, it's important to find out if they use staff musicians and, if so, how much they charge. Typically the charge is something around $100 per musician per hour. But note that some houses of worship charge even if you *don't* end up using their musicians—given the quality of some of them, it's probably worth paying not to hear them sing! If you want to hire a cantor, that's going to run about $150, choirs range in price from $500-800, and you can add a trumpet for $175. Plus don't forget the church "donation," say somewhere around $500. For one associate of mine, the suggested donation was $750, which included $200 for the organist/music director. I imagine many of these fees are non-negotiable (well, unless you are willing to risk eternal damnation. In that case, just don't mention my name).

Bait and Switch

Getting the Sound and the Players You Want

The key to booking music is to hear the band play or the DJ "mix," consider how much you like their sound, and then book those same professionals. In other words, make sure that the musicians you're fond of are the ones who will actually play at your wedding. Ascertain that the DJ you liked is the one who will be hosting your reception. This advice may seem obvious, but sometimes plans that start out very simple and straightforward can get a wee-bit complicated. Let me explain.

Suppose that you hear through the grapevine that a particular band is really good, so you call them up to ask for a demo CD or video, allowing you to give a careful listen at your own leisure. When you hear the music, the band sounds just great. Imagine you go ahead and book them for your special day. But somehow on the day of your wedding, the wedding band plays terribly. You're left, to quote that old song, "bothered and bewildered," wondering what happened.

What did happen? Well, it's our old nemesis, bait and switch. You think you're getting one commodity, only to be given something inferior when the deal is closed. In this case, recording studios, with all their fancy audio editing technology, can make almost anybody sound good (if you doubt this, go see Britney Spears performing live, sans lip-synching, assuming that ever happens). So you think you're getting a top-notch band, and you end up with something less than stellar. Now of course it's hardly surprising that a band will sound better on a recording than they will in person. But if you don't hear the band live, you'll never know how much worse the band can be. In my own case, I went to see a band live after hearing their promising recording of wedding favorites. Turned out that much of their sound was computer generated, which did not translate well in a reception hall ("Ladies and Gentlemen, before we introduce the bride and groom, please put your hands together for the XT-5000!").

Now let's consider another possibility. Let's say you hear of a band called WPM, which is hip lingo for "We Play Music." You decide to call them up and make a date to see them live. You like what you hear, so much so that you even introduce yourself to their lead vocalist, Joe Singer, who gives you their card. After thinking it through, you call the company and book WPM for your reception.

But hold on one minute! What you may not realize is that some bands are what are called "brand bands." In fact, it may turn out that the name WPM actually represents several bands consisting of various groups of musicians who adhere to the general style of WPM. So if you're not careful, you might intend to hire Joe Singer and his players, only to have Jim Vocalist and his own set of musicians show up, resulting in a musical performance that is rather different from what you expected.

Again it's bait and switch. In the first example you heard the same band perform well on tape but not in person. In the second instance you got an entirely different set of musicians! To be sure, on some occasions there may not be that much difference between Joe Singer and Jim Vocalist. After all, they do represent the same company. But I still say, why take the chance? Professional musicians will tell you that the sound of a band—what they sometimes describe as how "tight" the groups sounds—depends crucially on the particular mix of the particular players involved.

And lest you think this truth applies only to bands, it turns out that some large DJ companies that employ several crews are also guilty of this tactic. Of course, with a DJ the music itself will obviously not sound different, but the MC might. There are many different kinds of DJs, some of whom may appeal to you more than others (I'm sure we can all remember a wedding with a nightmare DJ—you know the one: He was just a little too into the Hokey Pokey). If you think you're hiring a certain DJ only to have someone else show up at your reception, that can certainly put a damper on the festivities.

How to Handle It

1. Hear the Music Live

As I mentioned, recording studios can make a band sound and look great. In fact, sometimes a group can sound good when it isn't even them doing the singing—anybody remember Milli Vanilli? So it's not enough just to give a CD a careful listen. I recommend taking the time to see a candidate band or singer live. And why not? It's fun to hear great music. Ask your contact with the band where they'll be playing in the upcoming month and go hear them. You can make a date of it. That's my tip not only for wedding planning but also for your marriage—make your errands into dates! With so many responsibilities and obligations that come with any relationship, why not turn every chance you get into a fun outing?

If you do get the opportunity to hear a band, you might try to do so in a venue that resembles your own. Hearing a band play a concert gig may not give you an accurate sense of what they'll be like at a wedding reception. On the other hand, if you do hear them at a reception and you don't like their song choices, you might consider another musical option, as many bands know how to play a certain number of songs well but don't do so well with novel requests. The band, or a DJ for that matter, may say that they are happy to add more variety but the likelihood that they will do something dramatically different is low.

In my case, my fiancé and I made two trips to see the band we ultimately selected. For the first trip, we attended a high school reunion where the band performed. (Surprisingly, none of the other attendees seemed to notice that we hadn't actually been members of the class of...what was it again?) But because we wanted to incorporate some Hebrew songs into our reception, we also saw a smaller gig at a synagogue. The first performance showed that the band could do large festive events; the second revealed their proficiency in the relevant second language.

Now that I have gotten you ready to put on your dancin' shoes, before you head out the door to listen to some music, here are some things to look for:

- ♫ Can the band play a broad selection to get all ages dancing? Everything from [insert name of old-time rocker who was once considered risqué but is now tame enough to appear at Superbowl halftime shows in the post-Janet-Jackson era] to [insert name of latest hip-hop artist to have sold more albums than any performer over the age of 30].

- ♫ Are they attuned to the audience, and can they switch styles if necessary to get people on the dance floor?

- ♫ Similarly, can they improvise when things come up, as they inevitably do? For example, can they change tempos during a father-daughter dance if is turns out that Dad is not as limber as he used to be?

- ♫ How loud is the music? Some bands are so loud you can't even hear yourself think, let alone talk to another guest.

€ Aside from the music, how do they work the room?
What is their style of announcing? Are they professional? If you have the chance, you might ask
them, "How will you announce our grand entrance
into the reception hall?" If they respond with
"Let's give a shout-out to the happy couple," find
another band.

2. Get Their Names in Writing

To paraphrase a lyric from Destiny's Child, "Get their name,
get their name!" Specify the exact musicians or DJ you want at
your wedding and write their names into your contract. Experts
also recommend calling a month in advance of your wedding to
verify everything. In addition, stay away from agents,
bandleaders, or DJ companies who will not guarantee who will
be at your reception. These folks allegedly exist to help musicians who don't want to bother with marketing or publicity.
They find bands in exchange for a 15 percent cut of what the
band charges. Similarly, sometimes wedding site coordinators
or catering managers at a reception site will demand fees for a
client to be listed on a site's recommended list of musicians.
The recommendations they offer may thus not represent the
best bands, just the ones willing to pay for advertising. Handle
this by asking coordinators if they take fees from recommended
musicians. If you don't get a straight answer, be careful.

It's not a good sign if the reception starts with this one.

Can you guess the most popular last dance song? That's
right, "Last Dance" by Donna Summer.

Play Your Songs

Before we move on, there is one other matter involving bait and switch that I should address. I have heard so many complaints from brides and grooms who requested certain songs—sometimes even producing lengthy lists of their favorites—only to have the band or DJ play something entirely different. Alas, I must include myself in this category. Yes, it's true: At my reception, our band substituted other songs for those that we had requested. For example, our second to last dance was supposed to be to Eric Clapton's "You Look Wonderful Tonight" but instead we heard "When a Man Loves a Woman." When this change occurred, my fiancé and I immediately noticed it, but our guests, of course, had no idea anything had happened, and the song worked fine. In fact, as a general rule, I like to say, "As the couple goes, so go the guests." In other words, if the bride and groom appear to be having a good time, then guests are likely to as well, no matter what minor mishap might be currently befalling the event. In fact, with regard to music, if you don't get exactly what you want, does it really matter? For the guests, certainly not—unless someone really had his or her heart set on doing the Macarena, in which case that guest probably shouldn't have been invited anyway. But for some of you, I realize it may be an issue (after all, is it really a wedding reception if at some point you don't get to dance to "YMCA" or "Shout"?).

How to Handle It

Although your band or DJ should certainly be willing to entertain your suggestions, I'd advise not going overboard in the request department. Although it's true that in a typical 4-hour set, musicians may play as many as 60 songs, it's best to reserve a few special numbers for key moments in the reception, such as your first dance, rather than attempt to fill every moment with your preferred music. ("Okay, when I stroll over to talk to my in-laws' wealthy business associates at Table 17, I'd really like to hear 'Lady in Red'" probably won't go over big with the band.) Keep in mind that you probably won't even hear many of the songs, especially if it's a large reception and you intend to spend even a couple of minutes chatting with each guest.

Consider also that if they are any good, bands and DJs may be better equipped to judge what music will work at certain points in the event. Experts admonish that sometimes the bride and groom like music that is so particular to them that it may not appeal to the majority of weddings guests. For example, I just love Latin music, and my first dance with my husband was choreographed to be a salsa dance. I eagerly requested more Latin music for the rest of the reception so that I could rumba and cha cha all night long. Well, if my band had listened to me, I'm pretty sure I would have been the only one out there dancing, as this was not a style that was familiar to most of my guests. Fortunately, the musicians were pros and offered a more eclectic mix than "Senora Kronzon" had initially desired.

Nonetheless, if there are certain songs that you want to be sure you hear at your reception, I have a couple of recommendations. First, make fewer requests (say, a maximum of a dozen songs) but be firm about those ones. You should make it absolutely clear that the all-important music to accompany such events as your first introduction as a couple, your first dance, the father-daughter dance, and your last dance should remain unchanged and ideally noted in writing on your contract. Second, you might consider giving the band/DJ a contingent contract, such that, God forbid, should they not be able to play "I've Had the Time of My Life," they should substitute Kool & the Gang's "Celebrate" (okay, feel free to mock my musical taste). In this way, you are giving the band or DJ options, which they'll appreciate, but the options are all ones that you approve of. So both of you will be happy with what ends up being played. And if there are songs out there that you absolutely hate, make sure that the band/DJ knows *not* to play those. "Achy Breaky Heart" anyone? Anyone? Finally, be sure to inform your band or disc jockey of any announcements you want them to make well in advance of the reception, and provide them with proper pronunciation of names. A poorly read announcement is often worse than none at all. Plan ahead to avoid embarrassment.

Timing

"Let's Get It Started!"

In a nutshell: Timing matters. Your band or DJ should not only know what to play but should know when to play it, that is, when to motivate the crowd and get the party going. After all, most of us want to have people dancing and just generally having a good time at a wedding. You don't want to have to worry about getting your reluctant relatives to the dance floor on your wedding day. In other words, you want a "Let's Get this Party Started" vibe, not "It's My Party and I'll Cry If I Want To." But some bands, or especially some DJs, think their only job is to play music—not true. They should know how to get people up and moving—think Richard Simmons, but slightly less annoying.

Keep It on Track

A second concern having to do with timing is to make sure that the festivities proceed somewhat according to schedule. You want the announcements to take place at the right time. You don't want things to drag (for example, a 3-hour dinner before dancing begins). Conversely, you don't want things to feel rushed (for example, racing through a best friend's serenade so that the cake can be cut. (For more on this debacle, go to Chapter 8 to see how my husband and I successfully combatted an instance of attempted time misman-agement.) And, for goodness sakes, don't have a dozen toasts in a row. There's only so much "Here, here" and "You go girl!" anyone can take. Spread out the love over the course of the event. Indeed, introducing each toast on its own adds to its impact.

Once you've constructed the schedule (for example, or-der of the proceedings, songs to be played at each event, and so on), give it to the band or DJ, go over it with them, and have extra copies available on the day. That way, even if things get temporarily derailed, you can easily get them back on track. At my wedding, the band threatened to devi-ate from the schedule and started asking for toasts at the wrong time (indeed, one of the toasters wasn't even in the room at that point). Fortunately, my mother whipped out a handy copy of the schedule and all was well again. Experts also recommend that you make sure that the band or DJ communicate with the reception hall staff, catering man-ager, and photographer so that every moment at your re-ception ends up unfolding in perfect harmony.

"All Night Long"

Lionel Richie sang about it. So did Jennifer Lopez ("DJ play that song...all night long"). They know what they're talking—or singing—about (at least when it comes to wed-ding receptions, maybe not so much about having a suc-cessful marriage). You want the party to go strong for long. But sometimes the musicians may get tired and, conse-quently, take extra breaks and even start winding up earlier than anticipated.

Make sure the band stays for the entire duration of time to which they've committed. Handle this by paying them their final amount only at the end of the event. As anyone who's ever tried to get assistance from a hotel desk clerk after already having checked out knows, "After the bill, you get nil."

Lowballing

What If You Want That Extra Hour?

Picture this: Everybody's dancing, having a good time. Even your minister's "gettin down." (Who knew he had such moves?) Suddenly the DJ taps you on the shoulder, saying (well, yelling really, given the volume of the party at that point), that he is getting ready to wrap up. You look at your watch and, sure enough, his time is up. But something's not right: Brides don't wear watches. Okay, what I mean of course is, how can the party end just when everyone is really starting to get into it and well before anyone has broken a heel, tripped over a chair leg, or even spilled wine on a designer gown? You check with the DJ, who gently reminds you (by yelling at the same decibel level as the launch of the space shuttle) that you booked him for only 4 hours. Your heart sinks: You'll have to end your party early. "Unless," chimes in the DJ, "you can pay me for an additional hour." "How much is that going to cost me?" you ask. "Only $500." Now you've got a big decision to make: Do you (a) cozy up to your rich mafia-linked uncle in the hope that that envelope he handed you earlier in the evening is only the first of many; (b) rush over to the gift table and try to figure out how many duplicate presents you'll have to hock to come up with the cash; or (c) send everyone home, perhaps by pretending to smell a gas leak (heck, it worked in the bridal shop).

Not a pleasant choice to make. It's called lowballing. You agree to the terms of a proposal, only to find out about some additional negatives after the fact (think bait and switch, but after the deal, not before). Just like some cell phone plans that sound attractive until you go over your allotted monthly minutes, some music providers intentionally offer a great deal on a limited amount of time, knowing that it's unlikely to be enough. They count on the fact that, when push comes to shove (or maybe bump comes to grind) you're not going to end everyone's fun, and you'll pay the exorbitant overtime fee.

Did You Know?

"The Dance" by Garth Brooks is a break-up song.

"I Honestly Love You" by Olivia Newton-John is about the ending of an extramarital affair.

"I Will Always Love You" by Whitney Houston is a break-up song.

And the Hokey-Pokey is a song for people who can't dance.

How to Handle It

1. Be Realistic About the Time

Think about all the times in your ceremony and reception in which you want music to occur—everything from the minutes leading up to your triumphal procession down the aisle to that last dance of the night, before you and your husband go off to start a new life together (one helpful hint: It's best to wait at least 24 hours before logging on to eBay to sell all those non-returnable bud vases and picture frames). How long is all of that going to take? Best to figure it out now and book your musicians accordingly. Many bands and DJs will typically book for four-hour slots; if you expect everything to last five hours, then make sure you settle that discrepancy up front. My own wedding ceremony was slated to begin at 5 p.m. and last a half hour, followed by an hour of cocktails (5:30 to 6:30), and then a four-hour reception (6:30 to 10:30). Thus the total projected duration was five and a half hours, and I booked my band according to that schedule.

Incidentally, I thought that 10:30 p.m., rather than, say, midnight, was a realistic ending time. After all, my wedding was on a Sunday, which definitely had its advantages: Not only are reception halls more likely to be available and less expensive than on Friday or Saturday, the same holds for bands and musicians. However, it did mean that many of the guests would have to get up and go to work the next day, so just as one can err by booking musicians for too few hours, I avoided the mistake and expense of booking them for too many hours. By midnight my husband and I were already in the honeymoon suite.

Incidentally, once you figure out the total amount of time for which you'll want music, there is no need to lead with this figure in your discussions with a band or DJ. Let them make the first move. Otherwise, if you indicate, for example, that you are looking for four hours of music, they may say that they typically play for only three hours but will play for an additional hour if you are willing to pay overtime. Never mind that the same individuals would tell someone who is looking for five hours that they typically play for only four. Remember: In any negotiation, whatever you tell the other side affects what they say in return. So my first piece of advice is don't feel like you have to tip your hand right away.

2. It's Time to Negotiate

Okay, but let's say you find a band that you really like and, before revealing that you want them for five hours, they tell you that their typical booking rate is for four hours. You might respond with the following:

"I am really looking for a total play time of five hours."

They may agree. But what if they want to charge a hefty overtime fee in return? In that case, you might try one of the following:

- ℄ Ask if they can waive the additional fee for you. This might be an especially effective ploy if you are booking for a non-Saturday event, when bands are more likely to be free—I mean "available"—nothing comes for free!

- ℄ Tactfully imply that you don't *have* to book that band: "I'm afraid that an extra $500 for the final hour is beyond my budget. I could go with another band, but I would prefer to go with you if we can work something out."

- ℄ Trade across issues. Your issue is that you really want music that lasts as long as your reception. The band's main issue is to obtain additional money. A compromise seems possible, in which each party gets a bit of what it wants: You pay the band an additional $250 (that is, half what they're asking, a reasonable amount). In return, they stay for the entire reception but get to take longer breaks in the middle (especially before the party really gets going).

You may end up paying something extra for that additional hour, but there are other potential charges you should simply refuse to pay. And if the band or DJ does not accept that, time to go with someone else. For example, avoid the following:

- ℄ Consultation charges.

- ℄ Extra charges for rehearsals. For my wedding, Andrew needed to rehearse with the band, but

they found time to do that during the setup and
cocktail hours (the latter occurring just with
the pianist, as he wasn't playing at that point
anyway).

𝄢 Special equipment charges. Unless it's essential that your reception look like a Las Vegas
show, I think you can skip the disco ball and
laser show, especially if the DJ wants to charge
a lot for those extravagances.

Contract Fundamentals

Finally, after you've booked your band or DJ, read the
contract carefully to make sure what was verbally promised
is, in fact, in writing. For example, my musicians agreed to five
and a half hours, including four hours of continuous music, but
the contract said three hours. It was probably an honest mistake.
Still, I took the time to correct it, and so should you. In addition
to the correct date, time, address, phone number, and deposit
amount, your contract should include:

𝄢 Name of DJ or band (including the DJ's assistant if one is furnished, and all band members
and the instruments they play).

𝄢 Length of time they will play.

𝄢 A list of required songs and substitution policy if
necessary.

𝄢 Suggested attire.

𝄢 The number of breaks and the length of time of
each (one source suggests a 15- to 20-minute
break after each 45 to 50 minutes of playing).

𝄢 Whether recorded music will be provided during
breaks.

- A list of special equipment that will be provided.
- A provision that setting up and breaking down time is included in the rate.
- All fees and overtime rates and policies.
- Cancellation/refund policy.

Now go have the time of your life!

Chapter Seven

Flowers

I believe that choosing the flowers for your wedding comes at a good point in the whole wedding planning process. By now you've typically passed some major booking milestones: You've chosen a location for the ceremony and the reception, picked out the gown you'll be wearing, and maybe even selected the band—or at least told your cousin that, sadly, the reception hall won't permit accordion music. You're probably dying for a break, a respite from the whirlwind of planning your nuptials. But who are we kidding? I know you feel like you still have much, much more to do to plan your day. So if you can't take a real break, go take care of the wedding flowers. It's time to, literally, stop and smell the roses.

Flowers are the element of a wedding that adds that air of elegance to your day. I was really excited to deal with this part of my wedding preparations, envisioning myself looking at pretty flower books and viewing beautiful floral arrangements and saying something like, "I want this flower and that flower and maybe a dash of this and a whiff of that." I admit it: I imagined it would be something like Michael Jackson going on a shopping spree as he did in that Martin Bashir television documentary a few years ago. At one point we saw Jackson, the sole customer, waltz through a posh Las Vegas home furnishings boutique, pointing to items almost at random, making purchases without even looking at the price tags: "I'd like that vase and that frame and...". Okay, I don't have Michael Jackson's money (in fact, if reports about his bankruptcy are true, neither does he), but I naively thought that when it came to wedding flowers, I'd have the financial wherewithal to play around with various combinations until something caught my fancy. After all, how much could flowers cost? Granted, when I started, I didn't know the difference between a Biedermeier and a boutonniere, but I figured nothing could be too expensive. After all, to paraphrase Shakespeare, a rose by any other name should cost the same, yes?

Boy was I wrong! There are inexpensive flowers and there are ridiculously expensive ones. For example, who knew that an arrangement of exotic birds of paradise will cost you approximately $75 for only 10 stems, but a bouquet of irises will run you less than half that price (around $30) for twice the number of stems? What's more, many florists don't let you just putz around in their botanical garden, as I had so innocently fantasized. Sure, you can look at existing arrangements in the store, as well check out picture books, but for the most part, florists like to communicate with you first before directing you to a particular arrangement. I found all of this intimidating. For example, one of the florists I met with immediately began firing lists of flowers at me, telling me which goes with which, and talking so fast I felt like I was in an episode of the Gilmore Girls. I didn't know what the heck she was talking about and felt utterly confused. So unless gardening is your hobby and you view yourself as the next Martha Stewart (without the rap sheet), you can get easily lost and manipulated into spending more than you'd like.

Entrapment: Flowers, Flowers Everywhere!

Which brings me to my first point: When you meet with various florists, beware of entrapment. Much like other elements of a wedding, flowers are something that we may be prone to buy too much of, spending more money than we should. In fact, the most common form of entrapment involves getting you to buy more and more flowers, causing you to splurge on vast quantities. But, unlike other elements of your wedding, the sales tactics used here tend to be rather subtle. Florists will not typically shower you excessively with flattery; there's no equivalent of "You look great in that dress!" ("You look great next to those flowers!" just doesn't sound as convincing). It's also unlikely that anyone will be completely honest and say, "I really think you should buy tons of flowers." Instead, florists will typically employ a more indirect approach, suggesting all of the places at your wedding site where flowers could enhance your nuptials.

I remember one florist in particular, who, as part of her sales pitch, suggested I put flowers in every available nook at the ceremony site. If I had followed all her suggestions, I would have needed pruning shears just to process down the aisle. For my reception, in addition to the standard centerpieces on each table, she wanted an arrangement on the piano and cake table. Then she wanted to place an arrangement next to the entryway, in the bathrooms, and even suggested placing a silk flower next to each place card. Fortunately, before she had a chance to suggest I wear a wedding gown made entirely out of white rose petals, I ascertained that she actually was not familiar with my wedding site. Here she had been suggesting all the locations that would be perfect for flower placements, and she didn't even know what the space looked like! It was apparent to me then that her primary goal was simply to sell me as many flowers as possible, whether they would look good at my particular wedding spot or not.

How to Handle It

I. Prepare

Preparation is vital to the flower-buying process. The process of buying flowers involves a bit of shopping around. I recommend that you go to a florist, ideally accompanied by an objective person and look around at the flowers there to see the kinds of arrangements they typically carry—do any catch your fancy? If so, then casually bring up the topic of weddings and ask what they have available (actually some sources recommend not even using the word wedding, lest the florist jack up the prices, but it otherwise might be a little more difficult to justify a bulk order—"mafia funeral" doesn't cut it any more).

Of course, if you have set up an appointment ahead of time, that works, too. Feel free to ask whether the florist is familiar with the location for your wedding, ask about his or her overall design philosophy, show the florist a picture of your wedding dress or bridesmaid dress (or a swatch of the fabrics) and maybe even pictures of flowers you ripped out of magazines to help ensure you're speaking the same language, and listen to the ideas the florist suggests. During this initial meeting, the florist will most likely come up with a list of possible arrangements you will need, including choices for bouquets, boutonnieres, and décor for the wedding, from which he or she will quote you an estimate for the price. That's your starting point for the negotiations. Of course, I suggest you visit several different florist shops, and keep in mind that flowers generally cost about 10 percent of the total cost of the wedding.

You will also need to scout out your location carefully to see where flowers would look best on your wedding day. For example, I was fortunate enough to get married at a golf club that featured beautiful forests, rolling hills, manicured lawns, and gorgeous landscaping. From the outset I knew I would not need to import many flowers because the setting already included so many wonderful natural elements. Similarly, Michael, a 27-year-old attorney, got married in a church during the Christmas season. (On New Year's Eve, in fact, which turns out to be one of the most popular days on which to get married—who knew?) This meant that many beautiful decorations were already present. So it's always a good idea to know what your site will already include before you think about adding more.

Indeed, before booking a wedding florist, I made a thorough inspection of the site where both the ceremony and reception would take place. Of course, sometimes such an inspection can be a challenge, such as if you find yourself planning your wedding during the winter for the following summer or you plan to hold a "destination wedding" and won't be visiting the site until shortly before you wed. And it's unrealistic to expect to try out various flowers in the room to see which colors and arrangements go with the décor, unless you possess unlimited time and money (in which case, feel free to skip ahead to the chapter entitled "Wedding Tips for People Too Rich to Read this Book").

But what you *can* do is take notes on the ceremony and reception rooms: Are there already flowers in the entryway, the hallways, or the bathroom? Should you put a vase on that piano in the cocktail room? What kinds of color schemes might work in the room? (When I inspected my site, I jotted down the room colors, noting the color of the walls, the carpeting, the tablecloths, even the ceiling.) Or better yet, take a picture of the relevant locations and think it over. You can also talk to the director of the site to help anticipate where flowers will be growing during the time of year when your wedding will take place. For example, by talking to the site director, I was able to learn that my wedding location would feature flowers bordering the outdoor path where I was going to process, along with several hanging arrangements, eliminating the need to adorn those spots with additional flowers.

Even if you can't tour your wedding site ahead of time, check to see if their staff can send you a photo or two from their publicity department. And if possible, book a florist who either is already familiar with your wedding site or at least is willing to check out the site before making recommendations. Such an expedition will enable your florist to prepare a list of the types of flowers and flower arrangements that will fit your location. I also recommend that you coordinate the flowers with your wedding attire as well as with the site. Spend some time thinking about which kind of flowers and bouquets will go with the look of your gown, the color of your bridesmaid dresses, and so on. Some experts, for example, recommend that large floral bouquets be reserved for simple wedding gowns and/ or sites that feature less ornate decorations. And, as I've mentioned, it's also a good idea to bring a picture of your dress and/or swatches of the relevant fabrics to your meetings with florists.

Doing such on-site research will be a great aid to you as you decide what constitutes an appropriate size order from your florist. Come up with a monetary figure associated with that size: this figure is your bottom line, and you should commit to it; having this figure in mind during your various meetings will help guard against any sudden temptation to order more flowers than you need. Table A offers an exhaustive checklist for wedding flowers you may like for your wedding; I encourage you to choose a subset of the items listed and use that as your guide.

Table A: Flower Checklist
(Courtesy of UltimateWedding.com)

Bouquets:

- Bride
- Maid (matron) of honor
- Bridesmaids
- Flower girls
- Bride's toss bouquet (separate for toss)
- Hair Ornaments
- Boutonnieres
- Mothers

Ceremony:

- Altar
- Chuppah
- Pews
- Main entrance
- Runner

Reception:

- Centerpieces
- Head table
- Staircase railing
- Buffet tables
- Cake table
- Place-card table
- Wedding cake top

Boutonnieres:

- Groom
- Best man
- User
- Father of bride
- Father of groom

Mothers:

- Corsage (lapel or wrist)
- Purse decoration flowers
- Arm bouquet

Hair Ornaments:

- Bride
- Maid (matron) of honor
- Bridesmaids
- Flower girls
- Junior Bridesmaids

2. Recycle

It may be possible to negotiate with your florist to re-use some of the flowers you have ordered, particularly if you intend to hold your ceremony in one location and your reception in another. For example, if a florist pressures you to purchase pricier floral arrangements, you can agree—but only if the florist agrees to let you move some of those arrangements from the ceremony site to the reception site after you have said your I dos, thus saving you the cost of unnecessary additional flowers.

Did You Know?

Life in the 1500s: Most people got married in June because they took their yearly bath in May and were still smelling pretty good by June. However, they were starting to smell, so brides carried a bouquet of flowers to hide the body odor.

If somebody hands you flowers at a wedding, they might be trying to tell you something.

Entrapment: Let's Import Flowers From Abroad!

A second kind of entrapment involves the kinds of flowers you buy. The fancier the flower, the more it's going to cost you. Even basic flowers can cost more if you are ordering them out of season. One source estimated that you end up paying 25 percent more if you want flowers at a time when they are not locally available and thus must be shipped in from elsewhere. So unless you're Britney Spears, who reportedly spent $100,000 for special white tulips from Holland for her wedding (mind you, the second in one year, for those of you scoring at home), it pays to be wary of florists who pressure you to order exotic flowers.

How to Handle It

1. Prepare

I know, I know: more preparation. But buying flowers requires a little bit of homework. Assume you've already gone on an expedition to your wedding site to see how many and what types of floral arrangements would be needed, along with preliminary schemes and colors. The next assignment involves studying the cost of flowers in general, and by season in particular. First, it's good to have a general idea of which kinds of flowers are less expensive, such as carnations and daisies, and which are more expensive, such as roses and lilies.

Second, take a few minutes to discern which flowers will be in season and which will be out of season. Poinsettia is obviously a winter plant and thus out of season in summer, whereas tulips are a spring flower and thus more costly in autumn. And don't count on the florist to tell you what's currently in season. When my friend Lori asked about some out-of-season flowers, the response was "We can get that for you." Over and over again. No mention of the added price for wanting summer flowers for a winter wedding. Not to worry, though: Given that a comprehensive list of popular flowers available by season is found in Table B, courtesy of *www.ElegantBride.com*, I'm certain you'll ace this assignment.

Table B: Popular Flowers (Courtesy of ElegantBride.com)

Spring flowers

- Apple or cherry blossoms
- Daffodils
- Dogwoods
- Forsythia branches
- Hyacinth
- Irises
- Larkspur
- Lilies
- Lilacs
- Lily of the valley
- Pansies
- Peonies
- Sweet peas
- Tulips
- Violets

Spring greenery
- Fern
- Ivy

Summer flowers
- Asters
- Calla lilies
- Dahlias
- Daisies
- Delphinium
- Geraniums
- Hydrangeas
- Iris
- Jacobs ladder
- Larkspur
- Queen anne's lace
- Roses
- Shasta daises
- Stock
- Sunflower
- Sweet William
- Zinnias

Summer greenery
- Fern
- Beech leaves
- Ferns
- Meadowsweet
- Stock
- Goldenrod

Fall flowers
- Asters
- Chrysanthemums
- Dried hydrangeas
- Gerbera daisies
- Marigolds
- Roses
- Statice
- Zinnias

Fall foliage
- Autumn leaves
- Rosehip
- Rosemary
- Yarrow

Winter flowers
- Amaryllis
- Camellias
- Forget-me-nots
- Jasmine
- Orchids
- Poinsettias

Winter accents
- Fern
- Ivy
- Pine
- Rhododendron leaves
- Spruce

Available anytime
- Baby's breath
- Carnations
- Gardenias
- Ivy
- Roses
- Snapdragons
- Stephanotis

Now, for some of you, learning that the flower you'd love for your wedding is out of season will mean not going with that choice, and that's fine. But what if you really want that flower? Maybe it's the same flower that your cousin had at her wedding, or maybe it symbolizes the first time your sweetie bought you something that didn't need to be plugged in. Well, then it's time to negotiate. I recommend proposing a trade-off: You'll pay for a more expensive flower if the florist will offer a discount on a bulk order of said flower. Alternatively, you can agree to pay more for a special flower but obtain some sort of guarantee in return. For example, after you ask what the price of the flower will be and the florist inevitably replies that it's expensive, you can respond with the following:

"I realize that importing flower X will be pricier. Can you offer me some guarantee that if I pay a higher price, it will actually be there on the day of my wedding?"

In this tradeoff you agree to pay a higher amount if the desired flower is, in fact, present in the bouquet on your wedding day. If the flower is mysteriously absent, you pay less. Using an "if-then" statement can often help here: For example,

*"If I am going to buy X flower
then I'd appreciate a discount on the vases."*

But before you negotiate, here's one other homework assignment for which you can earn extra credit: Ask around to determine which flowers are likely to wilt in the heat and which are likely to give off too heavy a fragrance. Experts recommend avoiding certain fragile flowers in the summer or in humid climates—flowers such as gardenias, lilies of the valley, tulips, and wildflowers. Instead, go with hardier varieties, such as zinnias, dahlias, lilies, and hydrangeas.

Bait and Switch: That's Not the Same Arrangement as the Picture in the Book!

If you don't engage in at least a little bit of the kind of research I've been describing, you may really get taken by your florist. The most popular way is through the bait-and-switch tactic, whereby a florist promises you one thing and then delivers something else.

For example, when I was planning my wedding, I recall visiting one florist whose shop was around the corner from my home. This florist's close proximity certainly made it easy for me to meet with her, but that did not mean that she would be easy to deal with. I recall that she deluged me with books showcasing designs that she claimed she could do for my wedding, all the while refusing to show me any arrangements that she had actually put together in the past.

And that's the problem with relying on books: Unless a florist shows you albums featuring his or her own arrangements, it is nearly impossible to determine whether that florist can recreate those beautiful pictures. In fact, it could even be the case that no florist will be able to replicate what appears in a certain book. Case in point: One floral expert explained to me that a certain bouquet of flowers I found in a Martha Stewart book simply could not be recreated, period. And it wasn't because that particular florist was not talented enough, but rather because of all the extra work that is done to flowers to get them camera-ready. But, of course, readers see it and expect a florist to be able to copy it. Then again, Martha's readers probably also used to expect that they weren't getting wedding advice from a convicted felon. Live and learn. The point here is that it's hard to know whether a florist can actually put together arrangements seen in books without seeing the hard evidence. If you rely on pictures in books, you may be in for a shock on your wedding day when the florist is not able to duplicate the arrangements you had picked out.

In some cases, florists won't honor your wishes at all, making up arrangements that bear no resemblance to what you ordered. That's awful, but pretty rare. More common is that you get fewer flowers in your arrangements than you expected, or you fall victim to the slight substitution: A florist goes with a different flower than the one you ordered, citing the fact that your preferred option is not in season and/or not locally available. Or you get the flower you wanted but, because of the aforementioned "season-region" problems, have to pay more for it, something the florist conveniently forgot to mention when you made your initial order. This is, of course, the ol' bait-and-switch tactic: You sign on for one type of flower, thinking it costs you X amount. Later you find out the cost is actually higher, say $X + Y$ dollars. ("Y" as in "Why am I paying this much more?!") Alternatively, florists may substitute a cheaper flower for the one you really desire. That way they get paid for the expensive flowers but provide the less expensive ones. Or a florist may eliminate that flower from your arrangement altogether!

A version of this last type of mishap happened to my friend Denise, who bought one set of flowers but received something different. Specifically, Denise said she wanted no lilies; I don't know why she was categorically opposed to them (maybe she's allergic?), but suffice it to say that she was the bride and it was her prerogative. On the day of her wedding, she saw lilies in her bouquet. And by then, it was too late! Come to think of it, maybe those tears I saw on Denise's face that day weren't tears of joy but, rather, disappointment with her bouquet— or, heck, maybe she was simply having an allergy attack—an allergy to incompetent florists, that is.

How to Handle It

1. Insist on Viewing the Flowers

You're less likely to be surprised by your floral arrangements on your wedding day if you view your florist's actual arrangements beforehand. At the bare minimum, you should look at books featuring pictures of *their* flowers (that is, not some generic flowers). Ideally, you should look at actual arrangements. Keep in mind that the florist may try to charge you for seeing a sample bouquet, or a sample centerpiece, or both. This presents an opportunity to negotiate. For example, if your florist wants to charge you to see a sample bouquet, you can agree, but only after you've secured a promise to get to see a sample centerpiece as well for no additional charge. If the florist refuses, you can ask for something more modest, such as the opportunity to view a simpler arrangement, and if even that doesn't work, you might find yourself another florist. Barring that, some experts recommend visiting other weddings that are serviced by the same florist; that will at least give you some idea of what you are likely to get.

All in all, these options are meant to let you preview some sort of preliminary version of your floral arrangements before the actual day. Unless the florist is a complete fraud, I doubt that the arrangements will differ greatly from what he or she shows you—after all, florists don't like to make more work for themselves. In addition, the more the florist sees how committed you are to the flowers, the more committed he or she is likely to become as well and thus more likely to do a good job for you.

2. Use a Contingent Contract

Seeing a reasonable facsimile of your flowers ahead of time should provide you with some reassurance that you won't be surprised on your wedding day. But you may want a guarantee in the contract, especially if the florist insists on the right to substitute flowers. If this happens, you'll want the substitutes to be truly comparable.

To guard against unacceptable flower substitutions, make what negotiation experts call a contingent contract, such that if flowers become unavailable, then only specific alternatives (ideally of equivalent quality) will be acceptable. For instance, for my wedding, the contract stated that "half of the tables will be decorated with *either* square glass containers of white dendrobeum orchids, white lilies, white snapdragon, cream roses, and cream hydrangeas decorated with chinaberry *or* square glass containers with pale cream dendrobeum orchids, white lilies, white snapdragon, cream roses, and white hydrangeas accented with chinaberry." I wonder if anyone could tell the difference?!

3. Just Put It in the Contract!

Finally, bait and switch can be handled by explicitly specifying key essentials on your contract. For example, mention the name of the florist who will actually deliver and set up the flowers. If you don't, the florist may assign somebody else to your wedding. Next, don't just list which flowers you want on your contract. List each type of flower, its color, and, crucially, the number of each in an arrangement. That way, the florist has to abide by the contract and if something goes wrong, you have recourse. Alternatively, you can be creative and pull out a pencil and draw the arrangement or these days, thanks to the advent of camera cell phones, take a picture of the arrangement. Other contract fundamentals are included at the end of the chapter.

Nibbling

With flowers, you should also be aware of many costs that may be added to your tab. I think it's okay for florists to explain, up front, what these additional costs are, but they should do so as early on in the process as possible. What's not okay is when you've been led by a florist to assume you've covered the basics of flowers for your wedding, only to find out you may have to pay an additional cost for what you really want.

Here's an example: A good friend of mine recently got married and wanted her guests to be able to take the center-pieces home. Her florist quoted her a price for the center-pieces placed in silver bowls of $75—a price that she was pleased with. What her florist did not tell her was that the silver bowls had to be returned at the end of the night. To be sure, the contract that my friend received did specify at the bottom that rented items (silver bowls, lighting, trees) are "the sole property of the company and are to be removed from the event locations by the Company or an agent of the Company only. All costs associated with missing items are the responsibility of the Client." This naturally prompted her to ask the florist, "How do the guests take the centerpieces home if the silver bowls must be returned?" The florist replied that taking the centerpieces home in the silver bowls would be fine—for an extra $10 per bowl.

My concern here is that if the florist knew in advance that my friend wanted to take the centerpieces home at the end of the night, why not tell her that the cost per bowl would be $85, not $75? Although such a response might seem more honest, obviously it appears to inflate the cost of the flowers so florists, like many vendors, tend to "unpack" charges, separating them so no one charge seems unreasonable (think a la carte menus at fancy restaurants). Such a practice also makes it more likely that the customer will agree to the final charge. As we've seen before, this practice is known as nibbling: Get the customer to agree to a price, commit to buying the item and then, just be-fore the sale, introduce an additional charge. In my friend's case, she had, at that point, already met with the florist on sev-eral occasions and essentially committed to the package. Doing an about-face because of a measly $10 charge per table is hard to do. As is so often the case, a little inertia goes a long way.

Unless you are careful, florists may nibble with regard to other "accessories" as well. They may charge a fee to provide such items as flower pots and planters; floral structures including arches, chuppas, and trellises; or lighting holders such as candelabras and lanterns. There could also be a delivery fee (my friend's was $300), as well as charges for the installation and breakdown of flowers (for example, 10 percent of the total price of the flowers) and other related items. (For example, decorative flower petals, special tablecloths, and so on.) There may be a fee for decorating the cake table with flowers or an extra charge for creating a mini-version of a bridal bouquet so you have something to toss. Some florists who are—shall we say—especially "penurious" may even charge an initial consultation fee to meet with them or charge to view a potential site with you. And if you want to preserve the original bouquet, it'll cost at lot: I received a quote of $400; plus you may well have to turn over the bouquet to your florist during the middle of the reception so that the flowers can be preserved while they're still looking their best.

And you thought European soccer fans were unruly...

The garter and bouquet toss

In parts of Europe during the 14th contrary, having a piece of the bride's clothing was thought to bring good luck. Guests would literally destroy the brides dress by ripping off pieces of fabric. In order to prevent this, brides began throwing various items to the guests, the garter belt being one of the items. Sometimes the men would get drunk, become impatient, and try to remove the garter ahead of time. Therefore, the custom evolved for the groom to remove and toss the garter. With that change, the bride started to toss the bridal bouquet to the unwed girls of marriageable age.

How to Handle It

First, you should be aware that nibbling may occur. That is, at the very least you should know in advance that there are possible hidden additional charges that the florist may add in later but not tell you about early on. So do your best to uncover these in advance. Indeed, if you are aware of a possible additional charge that has not been mentioned as yet, make a note of it, because chances are the florist will bring it up later. You can combat this ploy by holding something back for yourself, too, so that if the florist does spring something on you at some later point, you're prepared to bargain:

"You never mentioned the fee for watering the flowers; that's fine, but I expect a reduction in the transportation fee to compensate for this oversight."

A generally effective strategy for dealing with potential nibbling is to be direct: When you are ready to close the deal, say something such as,

"I want to verify that $X is the final price,"

or

"I want to verify that A, B, and C are included in the $Y price."

Such a statement implies that there will not be other costs added later. This way you are putting the burden on the florist to confirm the deal. Once he or she commits to a particular dollar amount, it will be harder to renege later and add on more. Such statements are preferable to more tentative questions such as, "Will there be additional charges later?" because such questions essentially imply that there *will* be more charges, perhaps even prompting the florist to invent additional costs.

If, in spite of your diligent preparation and use of declarative statements, you find the florist attempting to add another charge, don't immediately agree. I know it's hard, particularly after you've invested time and effort and had several meetings with the florist. But do not simply give in—after all, you have leverage: the contract has yet to be signed! Tell the florist there is an additional charge that you did not expect and that you expect that this charge will be removed. As mentioned previously, you can also play tit-for-tat by saying that, if the florist adds one more charge, you'll agree to it, but only if a comparable credit is added to the final bill. If all else fails, don't forget to remind the florist that he or she does not (in most cases) enjoy a monopoly and that you are certain that a competitor would be more than happy to have your business.

Contract Fundamentals

- Name and contact information for you and the vendor.
- Date, times, and locations of your ceremony and reception.
- Time and location the flowers will be delivered, time needed to set them up.
- An itemized list of the flowers you are ordering (include names of flowers, colors, number of flowers per bouquet or centerpiece).
- Substitutions if flowers are not available.
- Fees (if anything breaks, disappears).
- What the florist supplies (vases, bowls, stands, and so on).
- Cost and payment schedule (usually 50 percent).
- Cancellation/refund policy.

Chapter Eight

Photography *and* Videography

O f all the numerous wedding vendors with whom you'll be interacting, the one you'll have the longest relationship with is the photographer (indeed, if you are Liz Taylor, you may well have a longer relationship with the photographer than with Husband # ["insert large number here"]). You may find this idea surprising, as photographers are generally hired to record a single day, and if they are really good at their job, then you may not even be fully aware that they are standing there snapping shots of all the joyous moments from your special occasion. It may be the one time that it pays to have the slyest members of the paparazzi skulking around in the shadows, training their telephoto lenses on you. But when all is said and done, and when all of the other vendors have completed their services (skillfully negotiated by you) by the time of your wedding day, the photographer's job is, in some ways, just beginning. That's right: the photographer is the one vendor you will be meeting with after the wedding again and again as you go about organizing your pictures.

More specifically, once the photographer has taken all the pictures, you'll wait a few weeks to get the preliminary developed pictures (or proofs, as they call them) to view for the first time. Then you and your loved ones will spend some time deciding which pictures you'd like to order. That order will take time. Once the order comes in, don't forget to review the pictures and see which ones need further retouching, which will take some more time. At this point it's possible that other family members might want to submit additional orders for themselves. And if your relatives live far from each other, all this can slow the process down even more—although these days, many photographers will let you review the product online, which can be helpful if families do not live close by but have internet access.

In my case, my husband and I received the proofs shortly after our August wedding. Then it took me a little while to get the orders from my extended family. Given that my own parents live on the other side of the country and I didn't want to risk losing my precious pictures in the mail (after all, if you have structured your contract with the photographer properly, eventually you get to keep all the proofs), I had to wait for them to visit in October. When I finally put everyone's order in, I waited about two months for the photos, and then we met to fix problems with them a couple of times, so that by the time my perfect album was finished, I had been married more than a year!

Okay, so here are some basics about photography to get us started. In dealing with a photographer, there are a few essential elements to be discussed:

1. Proofs. These are the sum total of the pictures the photographer takes at the wedding, including candid and posed photographs.

2. Albums. These books contain all the finished wedding photographs. Prices run typically run from

$200 to $400, depending on how nice the album cover is.

3. Portraits. These are formal posed pictures that are typically taken before the wedding day. Or sometimes they are enlarged photos taken from the wedding proofs. On occasion the couple takes an engagement picture that is more informal, either inside or outside the studio, which can accompany an announcement in the newspaper. My photographer called this the "fun picture."

All told, the average cost of wedding photos is about $1500. And that doesn't count paying the ransom for the blackmail photos the best man took at the bachelor party.

Entrapment: Buy, Buy, and Then Buy Some More

As I've been hinting, a relationship with your photographer involves ordering pictures. Who doesn't want a lot of pictures of their wedding day? I know I did! And the photographer is happy to oblige: the more pictures you order, the better. But sometimes the photographer may try to get you to order a lot more pictures—more pictures than may even be in your best interest. Because let's face it: It can be hard to stop ourselves. After all, there are so many choices: wallet size, standard size, oversize; photos for parents, in-laws, grandparents, friends; mini albums, standard albums, albums so large they make *War and Peace* look like a leaflet...you get the idea. They even have enticing sounding names for the various packages: bronze, silver, or gold. Aren't you worth the gold package? Never mind that it may seem like an actual gold bar is cheaper than the gold photo package. And think about it, do you really need so many pictures?

Even worse, sometimes the photographer may trap you into buying a small set of pictures, knowing you'll want to order more later. For instance, you might be offered a low-priced package deal, say for a dozen standard size 8x10 photos as well as a dozen 5x7 photos for about a dozen hundreds ($1200). But if you want any more than that, the prices can be exorbitant. You may be asked to pay as much as $40 for each additional 8x10, and $30 for a 5x7. Even the *National Enquirer* might balk at prices like that for photos of Britney Spears in the arms of Bill Clinton.

Photographers also don't make it easy to compare prices from one studio to the next. It's like trying to buy a mattress: The reason that seemingly every store under the planet can guarantee the lowest price for a particular mattress is because apparently no two mattresses are exactly alike. Are there really that many different mattresses in the world? Unlikely, but good luck trying to convince a merchant of that fact while attempting to get a refund for a mattress that looks suspiciously like a dozen other cheaper models.

How to Handle It

So how are you going to negotiate for the best deal in wedding photographs—photos that you'll treasure for years to come? (I know I treasure mine, and I've even shown them to a few choice individuals, of course only after first having them put on sterile gloves). Here are some tips:

1. Negotiate for a Large Number of Proofs

Negotiate for a large number of exposures so that you get so many pictures you'll be happy with your allotment and there will be no need to be entrapped to buy more later. A minimum of 150 to 200 exposures are generally taken at a four-hour wedding. When I looked around, photographers were quoting prices for 200 to 300 exposures, making it seem as if they were giving me plenty of pictures. When I asked for more (yes, I really love pictures), they kept assuring me 200 to 300 would do. What was that nonsense? I knew I wanted more pictures!

Likewise, you too should not cave in. Shop around to various photographers and see which ones offer the largest number of proofs. My photographer assured me a range of anywhere from 300 to 800 proofs. This seemed tempting at first, because you think, "Wow, 'up to 800' is a lot." But let's be serious. If the contract says "300 to 800 proofs," which end of the continuum do you think that the photographer will lean towards? Will the photographer work harder when he or she can do less work for the same amount of money? It seems unlikely. So I offered the following compromise: "A range of 300 to 800 implies an average of 500—will you guarantee that number?" The photographer agreed and put it in the contract. The day my pictures arrived, I counted them. How many do you think I received? That's right: Just a handful of pictures above 500.

The lesson to remember here is that the vendor is providing a service to you; it's not like they love you and love your wedding and love to take pictures to their hearts' content. Nope. As a vendor, photographers want to secure clients; once the client is signed up, they typically want to do the minimum amount of work to satisfy their obligations as specified in the contract. Recall that my photographer knew that ideally I wanted more pictures than the minimum of 500 specified in the contract, but when push came to shove, he took only the minimum number he needed to cover his (as my grandmother would say) tochus.

I bring up this point to urge you to negotiate for more exposures because the more pictures taken, the more you'll feel like you have a complete record of your joyous day. And, like me, I imagine you'll feel happy you have so many pictures to help you remember your wedding. But there is another, more practical reason for ordering a larger, rather than smaller, set of proofs. The more pictures taken, the greater the likelihood that you will have ones that you truly love. Out of my 500 shots, there were only 50 truly beautiful pictures. And they *were* beautiful—much more so than if I had relied on a friend or guests with disposable cameras. The rest of the professional photos captured the event, for which I'm grateful, but they also look like anyone could have taken them.

The rate of one truly memorable picture out of 10 pictures taken is understandable. After all, it is hard, even for a professional, to take a perfect picture every time during the chaos that is a typical wedding. Sometimes someone's arm blocks the intended subject at the last moment, or one member of the bridal party looks great but another does not. I like to think of my husband and myself as fairly photogenic, but who knew how hard it is to get pictures in which we both looked our best? And that's just pictures involving us. What about pictures of the bride and groom with parents, siblings, and friends? The more people in the picture, the harder it is to get them all looking great.

The danger here is that this challenge of getting a good shot will not be reflected in the sample albums the photographers will show you during your initial visit. Photographers will try to deceive you into thinking most of their pictures are stunning. They will show you gorgeous albums filled with photographs so perfect they would make Ansel Adams jealous. What you don't realize is that those pictures may reflect only 10 percent of the photographer's exposures that day. Moreover, much work no doubt went into beautifying those shots. They were cropped, lightened, colored, airbrushed, and who knows what else.

So insist on seeing an entire set of proofs, not just the retouched ones, and spend a few minutes looking to get an overall sense of that photographer's work. Notice both the subjects of the photos (for example, it's probably not a good sign if everybody's eyes are closed and they're leaning over to get in the shot) and the quality of the work itself (it's also not good if, instead of closed, everyone's eyes are red and, although the shot is centered appropriately, everyone is white as a ghost). If it's possible to see photos taken at a location similar to where your wedding will occur, all the better. And you might bring along a friend or family member to lend an impartial eye.

Remember that it's wise to insist on getting as many proofs as possible to ensure that you'll get some great pictures. So shop around for the best photographer who offers the largest set of proofs. If a photographer does not agree to offer a substantial number of pictures to your liking, I offer you two suggestions. First, you can cultivate a little competition by telling the desired photographer that you "are interested in his or her services but want a larger number of proofs, such as the kind that [a rival photographer] is offering."

Feel free to use those exact words. But be delicate with the tone of your voice when you utter this statement. You don't want to appear too threatening or the photographer may simply tell you to go with the rival photographer, especially if he or she has many other clients. A second option at your disposal is to offer to pay a flat fee (for example, $400) for a large set of additional proofs not included in the original offer. That way, you get the additional photos you want, the photographer gets paid for them, and no one ends up haggling over inflated prices for each photo you desire over and above the original order.

Did You Know?

The term "tie the knot" goes back to Roman times. The bride would wear a girdle that was tied in many knots, which the groom had the "duty" of untying.

Shortly thereafter, the scissors was invented. Coincidence?

2. Negotiate for the Right Size Album

Here is a variant of the aforementioned strategy. Instead of negotiating to receive the largest number of proofs, think ahead about the type and, more importantly, the size of the photo album you desire. In particular, you might research the size of a typical album and then decide whether you want something larger or smaller. For example, if you are having a large wedding or just like looking at pictures of yourself like I do, choose an album with 80-100 photos. If you are planning a small wedding, you may need only 20 to 40 photos. If you establish these guidelines ahead of time, for example, that your album will be composed of X number of pictures, and your parents would like an album with Y number of pictures, you are less likely to be tempted to order additional photos at through-the-roof prices. Psychologists know that once people commit to something, they're less likely to do something different later (apparently psychologists haven't studied Britney Spears and and her propensity for 55-hour marriages). So select a package that offers a range of coverage that realistically tells the story of your wedding and hold firm to your selection.

3. Negotiate a Contingent Contract

Let's imagine that you now have a rough idea of the number of proofs you'd like, as well as the number of finished photos in the albums. And it's a good idea to keep this goal in mind so as not exceed your budget. At the same time there may be occasions in which you don't want to be trapped by this number. If you really want to leave your options open regarding the final size of your photo album, one way you can guarantee some flexibility is to make your contract flexible, or what's called a contingent contract. With a contingent contract, you don't have to worry about settling all the details until after the event has occurred.

You see, some people will be tempted to commit to a certain album size as soon as they sign with a photographer, and there are times when that is a good idea. However, it also means that when you finally get your pictures, you are stuck with them. But what if you want fewer photos than you originally anticipated? (because, alas, the makeup didn't hide the stress acne nearly as well as you thought, or, as happened to one of my friends, you were so heavily made-up that you didn't recognized yourself). Or what if, instead, you want a lot more photos? (because let's face it: you really did look hot that day). Making changes at this stage in the process could cost mucho bucks.

A better idea would be to sign with a photographer who guarantees some flexibility with your order or one who is wiling to extend a certain amount of monetary credit with your order rather than force you to immediately commit to purchasing a certain number of photographs. For example, for a total of $2500, I contracted to pay my photographer for his time and services, and he gave me a $1000 credit toward purchasing pictures. This sort of arrangement helps you in three ways: First, regardless of whether you initially order a specified number of proofs or not, they are only going to be ready for your inspection after your wedding, say three to four weeks after. So there is little advantage to ordering a certain number ahead of time. If anything, it might make more sense to wait and see how the proofs actually turned out before deciding how many to order. If they turned out terrific, maybe you'll want to order a lot, with many small sizes and some large. On the other hand, if they turned out, well, less than terrific, maybe you'll order fewer, but get larger sizes (or more copies) of the disappointingly small number of proofs that look great.

With my $1000 credit I was entitled to various combinations of photos. For example, if I wanted mostly large photos or if a relatively small number turned out to my liking, I could obtain approximately 30 8x10s and 3 5x7s (for a total of 33 photos). On the other hand, if I wanted a more equal ratio of large-to-small photos or if many photos turned well, I could get around 11 8x10s, 13 5x7s and 16 4x5 photos (for a total of 40 photos). I decided that what worked best for me was an elegant book containing only 8x10s for my primary album. As for my remaining 400-plus photos? I placed these additional smaller sized 4x5 and 5x7 photos in several separate albums. Thus, the contingent contract granted me the flexibility I wanted. At the same time, it provided an incentive for the photographer to try to take many good pictures in the hope that I would purchase more than the initial allotment speci- fied under the credit. I'll leave it to the reader to guess whether or not I purchased additional photos, but I'm confident that by the end of the chapter, you'll have a pretty good idea what I did.

The second way a contingent contract aids you is that the X amount you are given as your credit can serve as your bot- tom line. It is a clear reference point to tell you to spend that precise amount on pictures. Beyond that, it's going to cost you to add pictures to your album.

Third, it will normally take nearly a month for your proofs to be ready for inspection. Let's say you then take a few weeks to examine them and decide what to order. It's now two months since the wedding. Financially, this delay can be advantageous. Because, trust me, the longer the time away from the wed- ding, the less likely there will be money burning a hole in your wallet or a yearning burning in your heart to buy more pic- tures. I recall that after I returned from my honeymoon, I couldn't wait to see the wedding pictures that my family mem- bers had taken. I was jumping for joy, delighted to see how I looked as the bride with my groom. I poured over the pictures for hours that day. The second and third day, I still looked at them but by now was familiar with how the wedding looked in pictures. By the end of the week, my husband started coming up with excuses, such as needing to clean the house, so that he wouldn't have to look at them again. Hmm...while writing this, I just remembered that my kitchen floor needs washing: Maybe I'll drag the photos out—"Oh, Sweetie...." In any event, after another week, I too, put the pictures aside.

So you can see how a time lag can help to reduce our immediate desire to order more and more photos. Remember, on top of the month-long wait for the proofs, coupled with perhaps another month to order pictures, the completed photos will take on average at least another four months to arrive. So by the time your wedding album is ready for viewing, you will have been married for anywhere from six months to a year. By that time, it's likely that your excitement about your wedding day may have cooled a bit. If other marriage-related aspects of your life have cooled by then as well, it may be time for Dr. Phil....

4. Put It in the Contract

Finally, it's a good idea to include language in your contract specifying that (1) the original proofs will be handed over to you after a certain amount of time (such as after you've put in your order for finished photographs) and (2) the negatives will also be handed over to you at a particular time. My photographer agreed to give me the original negatives two years after my final orders had been submitted. That means that in two years I will have the originals for the rest of my life. (I'm counting the days!) And after that I can do whatever I want with them (maybe a photo spread in *Modern Bride*? Okay...maybe not). So if you are willing to be a little patient, you too can guarantee to have your originals for a lifetime! You can even use them to wallpaper your bedroom if you like.

Timing and Deadlines

When to Take the Pictures

Let's face it: the reason you want pictures of your wedding is not just to help you recall the joyous occasion (it's not even to help capture the best man stealing wedding gifts—or is that just an urban legend?). If you're like me, the reason to have wedding photos is to savor for years to come how you look in those pictures. I ask you, what's the point of pictures if they don't make us look good? Toward that end, it's ideal to time the photo session for when you look your best. So it's a good idea to put some care into when you schedule pictures. For example, assuming you don't hire Christina Aguilera to do your makeup, you are likely to look your best right after you've put on your makeup, had your hair done, and, of course, put on your killer dress. Ideally, then, I encourage you to take some pictures as soon as possible after that. Not only will you look great, but such a schedule will allow you to spend more time with your guests.

My friend Gayle told me that she wished that she had taken more formal portraits early in the day because after the ceremony, she faced a zealous photographer who was constantly pulling her away from guests—guests who, in some cases, had come all the way from Argentina to see her on her special day. Had she taken more shots before the ceremony, she might have been able to enjoy more time with her family and friends. Although some brides and grooms might be too anxious to sit for photos before the ceremony, personally, I thought it was romantic to take pictures with my intended before our wedding. It gave us some time to appreciate each other while posing a little before the hectic day truly began! In fact, some couples later report this was their favorite part of the entire day.

Notice that while this timeline ensures that your pictures capture you at your best, it does mean that you will most likely see your future spouse in advance of the ceremony. If your philosophy is not to see your soul mate until the ceremony, that's fine (assuming, of course, you don't mean that cute doctor sitting in the fifth row of the church). I still encourage you to take some pictures, which can be "portrait style," that is photos featuring just the two of you—by which, of course, I mean you and your dress—right away. Then, after the ceremony, you can freshen up and spend about an hour taking additional pictures, though you don't want to make your guests wait too long. And just be sure that if you're at a country club, you don't wear high heels on the golf course—turns out they don't like that. (Who knew?)

How Many Hours of Photography?

A second consideration is the number of hours to employ your photographer for your special day. Many photographers will want you to sign them up for a pre-specified number of hours. Although this is often a standard practice, sometimes photographers will intentionally underestimate the number of hours for which you'll need their services. Then, when the day arrives and you really want them to stay a bit longer than the pre-arranged number of hours so that they're sure not to miss Aunt Zelda leading the chicken dance (after all, such an event requires that she first ingest several hours' worth of cocktails), they will often agree to stay but end up charging an exorbitant price for that extra hour. That's a charge I don't want you to have to pay.

Here's a more realistic example: Let's say that your wedding runs from 4 p.m. until midnight. A photographer may offer a 4-hour time slot, say from 3 p.m. to 7 p.m. The start time is an hour before the wedding because you and/or the photographer may want to take pictures before the ceremony. Let's assume the ceremony lasts somewhere from a half-hour to an hour and then another hour is devoted to cocktails (or longer if Aunt Zelda has her way). Right there, you've spent a minimum of two and half hours. That leaves 90 minutes of reception time for the photographer to capture wedding toasts, cake-cutting, and, of course, dancing. You may be thinking, "Fine. If you've seen photos of one dance, you've seen them all." Well, not necessarily.

If you just want to capture the essentials of your day, four hours' worth of photos may be good enough. But the point of this book is to show you how to get the wedding of your dreams, not one that is merely good enough. There may be many memorable moments that take place during the latter part of the wedding festivities (especially if you have an open bar) that you will not be able to capture for posterity if you don't have the photographer around (assuming, of course, you want posterity to see the expression on your face just before the groomsmen throw you into the hotel swimming pool at midnight). Such events might include line dancing, the groom serenading his bride, the bride tossing her bouquet, guests saying goodbye to the happy couple, the bride's older, unmarried sister nursing her sprained ankle after diving for the bouquet, and so on. So, if you only contract for 4 hours of photos, you may miss some of these spontaneous Kodak moments.

To be sure, many photographers may try to prepare for such a contingency, but unfortunately, they may do so by rushing along all the reception activities to ensure that they fall within the critical 90-minute picture-taking window. In other words, photographers may try to fast-forward the wedding because they know that their time is running out, and even though they are also aware that you'll want pictures of all the important happenings, they're anxious to go home. With this option, you may well get pictures of everything, but it's unlikely that you'll be enjoying much of it, as you and your guests are raced from one activity to the next. In short, an overanxious photographer could ruin your wedding.

I faced a bit of this challenge at my wedding. The order of events at my reception called for, at one point, my "Guy of

Honor" (who also happens to be my coauthor) to serenade me and my husband with one of my favorite songs (Gershwin in this case—Andrew clearly has many talents!), followed by the cake-cutting ceremony. When the time came, however, I recall that Andrew was in the middle of his song when suddenly I felt the photographer try to steer me to a pose beside the cake, hoping to hasten along the cake-cutting portion of the evening. I remember thinking that I had to make a choice: Should I take the picture and start cutting the cake, which would mean that I'd miss some of the song? Or, alternatively, should I respect Andrew by devoting my attention to his lovely voice (at this point in the book Andrew would like to make it known that he is available to sing at your wedding reception for a nominal fee) and delay the cake-cutting by a mere five minutes? It seemed like a no-brainer to me! I immersed myself in the song, even swaying a bit to the music, thus making it that much more difficult for the photographer to beckon me towards the cake. The photographer had no choice but to wait! For which Andrew remains grateful to this day.

How to Handle It

1. Chance It

For all you risk-seekers out there, you may wish to chance this one. If you really think that you will need only X hours of photography, then by all means do not book X+Y hours. (Sorry. Andrew's a big fan of algebraic formulas!) If need be, simply extend the photo portion by an hour or two on the wedding day. Just be aware that you may be charged an arm and a leg for that extra time.

2. Choose a Package With a Long Time Span

Choose a package that includes a longer time span, say something like six or eight hours. Or better yet, hire a photographer who promises to capture the entire day. I advise you to shop around and ask photographers to indicate how many hours are covered by their service. If the photographers you visit all offer an insufficient number of hours, you'll need to negotiate. Specifically, tell them that you really are interested in coverage for the whole night and wonder whether they might provide that option. If they agree, great. But make sure there will be not be an extra charge, by saying something such as,

> *"I understand there will be no additional*
> *fee for the whole night, correct?"*

If they want to charge you extra, that could be all right too, depending, of course, on the price. In fact, I advise you to calculate what would be the total price for said services and weigh that against the other photo options you are considering, as well as the quality of the photos you think you'll get with a particular photographer. It could be that the price is comparable to competing offers or even slightly more expensive but worth it because the photos promise to be amazing. Take your time to make these calculations. If need be, tell the photographer that you need time to think about your options. It might even be the case that when you speak again, she or he will have come down in price, so be sure to check: As negotiation experts have noted, often times the only way to get a lower price is to ask for one. So remember: A little persistence goes a long way!

3. Try a Little Door-in-the-Face

If you want to secure additional hours of photography but don't want to pay for the whole day/night, here's a negotiation tactic you can try. It involves what psychologists call the "door-in-the-face" technique. Basically, you start off by asking for something unreasonable—something that is likely to be turned down by the other side, who (hopefully only metaphorically) slams the door in your face—and, then, after having been rejected, you come back with something that is somewhat more reasonable. The other side is likely to reciprocate and end up acceding to the more reasonable request, which they would not have otherwise done had your request not just followed a more unreasonable one.

So in this case, you might start off by asking for the entire day/night's worth of photography at the "four-hour" price. If the photographer accepts your terms, great. If not, that is, if the photographer rejects your offer as expected, you can respond by requesting six hours of photos at the four-hour price, something you wanted all along. The idea here is that by reducing your demand from wanting a photographer for the entire night for a low price to wanting a photographer for "a mere" 6 hours at the same price, you seem like you are making a concession. Because of a strong norm of reciprocity in our culture, the other side generally feels obliged to respond to your concession with a concession of their own, such as agreeing to the 6 hours you secretly wanted in the first place! Voila!

One final note: Just as the photographer should watch you to know when to take those perfect candid shots, so you should keep an eye on your photographer. Even when you hire photographers for a full day as I did, they may still try to rush you through pictures because they get tired and want to take breaks. On my special day, I was insistent that we take some pictures outside. Again, I'm from California, I love the outdoors, and the whole reason we booked a golf club for the reception was to enjoy the beautiful vista of the rolling hills. In our meeting prior to the wedding, the photographer agreed to my request for outdoor shots. In addition, on the day of the wedding, I repeated my request and my photographer assured me that we'd take some outdoor shots after the salad course.

Well, fast forward to just after the salad course, and I can't find the photographer and his assistants anywhere. I looked around, and even asked my parents to help in the search. By this time, dusk was settling in, and I really wanted my pictures before it turned dark. Finally I caught sight of the photographer leaving the reception room, entering a small vestibule. My now-husband and I quickly followed. But just as we entered the room, they fled toward a third room. It's as if they were running away from me, the crazed bride, and we were chasing them from room to room. Finally, we found them and they agreed to follow through on their commitment. We stepped out onto the green and golden grounds and took a handful of pictures just as the sun was going down. In fact, these outdoor pictures turned out to be the most beautiful of all of our wedding pictures. Imagine if we had missed our chance. (Actually, the groundskeeper might have preferred that to fixing the holes inadvertently made by my high heels.)

In short, try to keep on top of your photographer to ensure that she or he follows the prearranged schedule. Or better yet, delegate this task to a trusted friend. For me, pictures are (nearly) everything, so they were easily on my mind. But if you don't want to think about these things, ask a parent or friend to keep tabs on special concerns such as this one for you. Heck, isn't that what your maid-of-honor is for, anyway?

How to Get Your Photos Earlier After the Wedding

Let's say you just got back from your honeymoon. You're dying to get your hands on your pictures. You call your photographer but, "surprisingly" can't reach him as easily as you could prior to the wedding. Or imagine you've ordered the pictures you want and have been told that they will be ready by a particular date. Now that date has come and gone, but you still have not received the pictures. A fluke? Unfortunately, I think not. What I do think is that the photographer has finished the picture-taking portion of his job and now may be a teeny bit less interested in you and a wee bit more interested in attracting other potential clients. From a negotiation perspective, we observe that the photographer has more power in the relationship than you. Before you signed on with the particular photographer (and even up to the wedding day), you had nearly all the power. Post-wedding, however, the tables have turned. Photographers know that after the wedding, you essentially have no choice but to wait patiently (or, sometimes, impatiently) for your pictures, meaning they can take their time returning your calls and preparing your photo album.

How to Handle It

1. Hold Something Back

If you can, withhold the final payment until the process is complete, or at least nearly complete. In other words, break up the lump sum payment to your photographer into several payments, with delivery of those payments based on tasks accomplished. For example, you might make a first payment upon signing, a second payment after the wedding, and a final payment at the time of receipt of the completed album. Otherwise, trust me, once the vendor has received payment, he or she will lose much of the incentive and motivation to meet any further obligations to you. A schedule, with specific due dates for deposits and final balance payments, will serve as a carrot or reward for each step the photographer takes toward completion of the contracted services.

2. Be Specific

Specify in the contract the exact dates that the proofs and final album will be delivered. That way, you have grounds for action if the photographer does not meet specific deadlines.

3. Be Persistent

If all else fails, use the same strategy that one of my friends uses when, inevitably, his health insurance provider screws up the paperwork and refuses to pay a medical bill: call and call again, politely but assertively reminding the other party of their prior commitment and their need to meet their contractual obligations. Indeed, if you start to receive excuses, deflect them by uttering a short acknowledgment and then repeating your demands in a succinct matter:

You:	"I'm calling to see if my photos are ready."
Photographer:	"I am very busy and haven't been able to get to your order."
You:	"I understand that you are busy, but I would like you meet your contractual obligation to me."
Photographer:	"I have several customers who have been waiting longer for their pictures."
You:	"I realize that you have other customers; I would like my photos to be delivered by the date specified in my contract."
Photographer:	"I am going to have to put off other orders in order to fill yours on time."
You:	"I appreciate your situation, and I thank you for completing my order on time."

Bait and Switch

As noted earlier, sometimes you may sign on with a vendor to provide a particular service, only to find that the vendor may later try to change the terms of your agreement. Photographers are certainly not immune to this bait and switch technique. Let me give you an example: When my friend Sherry signed a contract with her photographer, like my contract, it included a $1000 credit toward the purchase of pictures. That amount could be spent in several ways, and the photographer showed her a chart quoting prices for pictures in various amounts and of different sizes. The pattern was such that the more total pictures she purchased, the larger the discount she'd receive. So if she purchased anywhere from

1 to 35 pictures (to quote Alicia Silverstone's character from *Clueless*: "As if!"), she'd pay $42 for each 10x10 photograph and $25 for each 4x5. But if she bought more than 120 pictures, the cost of each 10x10 would drop to $38 and the cost of a 4x5 would similarly drop by $4 to $21. In their conversation, the photographer offered the 120+ pictures package, suggesting that that would enable her to receive the largest discount available. She was pleased with the quoted discount and asked to put this information in the contract. Let me tell you that she's thankful that she did because months later, when it came time to order the pictures, the photographer conveniently forgot that he had promised this discount and started to quote much higher prices.

What the photographer was doing was bait and switch. He committed to a discount to get Sherry to give him her business. But after she was committed to the deal, he tried to change the conditions and forego the promised discount. His strategy was presumably based on the assumption that either (1) she would not get the discount in writing and/or (2) she would forget about the discount (again, "As if!").

This bait-and-switch tactic can be used in many different ways by the same vendor. Here's a second example: Imagine that you sign up with an employee of a photography company, assuming that he or she will be the photographer on your wedding day. But after the contract is signed, the company turns around and assigns a different photographer to your event— one whose work is not familiar to you. To take a third illustration, photographers may show clients their past work in beautifully bound leather albums. Customers get the impression that they too will have their pictures ensconced in fine leather. But the photographers neglect to mention that their packages come with cheaper vinyl albums with plastic covered pages. After the wedding, they suddenly remember to tell you that leather albums can be had for an additional fee.

Who said crushes never last?

Two out of five people have married their first love.

How to Handle It

1. Prepare

First, it's a good idea to prepare a list of elements that you want to include in any agreement with a photographer. (For example, include prices, preferred album covers, delivery date, and so on.) Then, you should make sure that you ask your photographer about each and every one of these elements. After you agree to each of the terms, do not leave the photographer's office without a contract that puts them in writing. As some of us know, all too painfully, the vendor may otherwise change the terms in his or her favor. But when you have a contract, should the vendor try to pull a fast one on you, simply point to your contract and smile!

2. Seize the Opportunity

If the photographer attempts to change the conditions on you, obviously your first recourse is to point to the contract, making clear what his or her obligations are. However, this may also represent an opportunity for you, in that if the photographer wants to change the terms of the agreement, there may be occasions in which it could behoove you to do so, provided you can gain something in return. For example, if the photographer wants to push back the delivery date, you might agree to the change, but only if additional photos are included in the final package at the price originally agreed upon.

Nibbling

As we have spelled out in other chapters, nibbling occurs when, just before a deal is sealed, the other side in a negotiation makes an additional request that in and of itself seems small. This tactic generally works at the end of long negotiations, in which you end up agreeing to the request because you are tired and don't want to spoil the deal or the nature of the relationship. But note that the other side gets this small concession for free, without having to give up anything in return. My photographer used this tactic near the end of our discussion, when we had already settled on the basics of our photo package. At this point, I mentioned that I wanted him to take photos of groups of guests seated at each of the tables in the reception hall (okay, I admit it: I wasn't above a little nibbling myself). He initially refused, saying that such shots would cost extra. Presumably he assumed that because we were so far into the contact negotiation, I would simply cave in and agree to pay more. But instead I mentioned that this feature of the photo package was critical to me, essentially implying that it was a deal breaker, and he agreed to include it in the original contact.

Another way to deal with a situation such as this is to inform the photographer that you will agree to his additional fee, provided he grants you a nibble of your own. For example, if you don't think you will need to order many photos of large groups, you might agree to pay an additional fee for such photos if and only if the photographer agrees to a 10 percent discount on photos of the wedding party or provides an extra hour of service for free (this is where you can get creative!).

Liking

As I've suggested throughout this chapter, it's important that you like your photographer because you will likely spend more time with this vendor than any other. The florist provides flowers and leaves, the caterer sets up the food behind the scenes, but the photographer interacts with you all day for picture taking, and then meets with you again on several follow-up occasions. So make sure that you like the photographer you're dealing with because you'll be dealing with him or her a lot. Ideally, choose someone who not only takes good pictures but someone who isn't so inconspicuous as to miss key wedding-day moments or so aggressive as to be too intrusive on your special day.

How to Handle It

Build a Relationship

Work to build a relationship with a photographer. Don't book any at your first meeting; go several times and see who is consistently responsive to your needs. I suggest that during these meetings, you highlight areas in which you have something in common with the photographer (for example, you come from the same religious background, you grew up in the same neighborhood, you are friends with another client, and so on). The goal is to have the photographer see you as more than another customer, that is, as a special client. If a photographer holds you in high regard, he or she is more likely to go the extra mile and do a superior job with your wedding.

In other words, try to make the photographer as invested in the relationship as you are. You might cultivate that relationship by hinting that you might order many photos. (Because you are part of a large family, or in my case, because you simply must have lots of pictures—this is one relationship in which it's okay to appear needy!) In other words, even if you do not plan to order any more than the minimum package offered, no need to let the photographer know that. It's okay to be a "photo-tease" because if a photographer senses that you are a cheapskate, he or she might feel a bit freer to be sloppy with the work. If you end up ordering fewer pictures than the photographer anticipated, well, that is your prerogative. And, by then, the pictures will already have been taken with good care.

But just as you are making use of the liking principle with your photographer, be aware that the photographer may be using this same tactic with you. For example, my photographer seemed so likable and friendly that I almost felt bad about pressing him to include what I considered to be essential elements in the contract. This is a common response: We don't want to do anything that might damage the relationship with the other party. However, just as with the other wedding service providers, your photographer is being hired to take pictures, not to be your friend; that's why you have bridesmaids!

Contract Fundamentals

Photographers often offer nonstandard contracts, making it very difficult to comparison shop. For example, one package will offer many hours of service on your wedding day but few photos (or only small-size photos) for your album. Another package will specify that an album will include X number of pictures taken from the proofs, but neglect to mention how many proofs will be shot throughout the wedding. So you may find yourself confused, preferring the number of hours that one photographer offers but also being attracted to the number of proofs offered by another and the price of yet a third photographer. Don't be deterred. It may seem like apples and oranges, but remember that you are still dealing with fruit (that is, it's not apples versus crackers). Take the time to compare the packages. As I suggested earlier, you might start by carefully imagining what you want your finished album to look like. For example, do you want a simple book of 10x10s, with one photo per page or perhaps you want to intersperse single photo pages with smaller pictures, say two to a page. Then see what your preferred album would cost you if provided by different photographers. Remember you want to get the best quality for the amount of money you are willing to spend.

In short, here are some specifics to include in any wedding photography contract:

- The name of the actual photographer who will be at your wedding.

- When the photographer will arrive and how long he or she will stay.

- The minimum number of shots that will be taken at your wedding, along with an assurance that those proofs (and the negatives) will eventually be provided to you to keep for ever.

- A specific schedule that includes due dates for deposits and final balance payments.

- The precise delivery dates for the proofs and final album.

- A date by which the negatives and proofs for nondeveloped photographs will be given to you for keeps.

- Any additional charges for travel time, overtime costs, or other fees (for example, reorder fees if relatives want copies but are unwilling to commit to a number at the time the contact is signed).

- A contingency plan in the unlikely event that the photographer cannot make the wedding.

Do you really need this last item? According to *SmartMoney.com*, you do: They report that Fireman's Fund has perceived a sufficient need to offer "Weddingsurance," which will supposedly pay for you to recreate key elements of your wedding, including flowers, cake, reception hall, and the wedding party itself, in the event that something goes wrong and you don't get photographs the first time. (I assume it costs extra to get Brad Pitt to play the part of the groom.)

Remember that I recommend that you make the contract contingent. That is, do not specify the exact number of prints and the type of album you intend to purchase. Instead ask for a monetary credit so that the photographer feels more motivated to take a lot of pictures!

Also include specific instructions of whom you most want to have pictures taken (for example, Mom, Dad, Mom and Dad, Mom and Dad and siblings, crazy Aunt Zelda, and so on), where the photos should be taken (for example, getting ready at home, outdoors, indoors, by the spiral staircase, on the dance floor, and so on), and which type of pictures you want (for example, candid or natural [known in the field as "photojournalist" style]; formal or "posed"; color; black and white; and so on). Make this list very explicit. The more explicit your instructions to the photographer, the greater the likelihood that he or she will give you want you want—after all, there is a written document that you can point to.

In fact, bring a copy of these instructions to the wedding, in case the photographer forgets his or her list. I even encourage you to spend a little time online looking at sample wedding shots (each photographer's Website should have them). Print out different poses you like. For example, I gave my photographer an actual compilation of pictures from other weddings that depicted fun poses that I wanted, and I even instructed him that I desired one of my husband kissing me under my veil. When it comes to pictures, I'm a hopeless romantic!

Videography

On your wedding day a photographer is a must. It's a rare wedding where you will not see a photographer (unless you are a Hollywood star, in which case you can be confident you won't see the photographers because they're hiding in the bushes). And it makes sense, right? I mean, who doesn't want a photographer to capture special wedding moments that you and your spouse can treasure over the years? So photographs are essential, but what about a wedding video—is that necessary? I believe it absolutely is. Let's see why.

I've been to several weddings in which the bride and groom felt that paying for a professional videographer was an unjustifiable expense. They reasoned that if they could cut costs by foregoing the video, then why not? Other people, like my good friend Denise, thought they could save on paying for a videographer by having a family friend record the event. Well, let me tell you that I wasn't the only person at the wedding who didn't remember seeing the videographer: the designated videographer himself also forgot and neglected to record the event. Let's just say that I think these days Denise refers to him as a "former" family friend.

It's true that in many cases a good friend will come through for you and record the day, but I doubt that the result will typically be the masterpiece you'd like it to be, simply because friends typically lack the skills of a professional videographer. For example, in one case I know of, a family friend with a penchant for capturing candid exchanges attempted to record a wedding by holding the videocamera down by his side and convincing everyone that he wasn't actually filming. Well, he might as well have not filmed, given that all he captured were folks' feet. I suppose there is some foot-fetish Website willing to pay top dollar for such a find, but I can't think of any other value to the tape.

What I am trying to say is that, prior to a wedding, a professional videographer may not seem so essential to you. But afterward, folks who forego it generally sing a different tune. In hindsight, they regret that they do not have a high-quality video story to chronicle their special day. As psychologists know, in the long run we tend to regret inaction more than action. In other words, we are more likely to regret not hiring a videographer than hiring one.

Now I know what you're thinking: "If I want to hire a videographer, might I fall prey to an unscrupulous entrapment scheme?" After all, the video option is often presented by a photographer as an additional service that one can order just before signing on the dotted line. In that case, maybe you're worried that the videography option really just constitutes a ploy by the photographer to get more money out of you. If you did have that thought, I applaud you for thinking like a negotiator. But I must say that I do believe that a videographer is a vital addition to a wedding.

Take my own wedding. Not only did the videographer capture key moments that I wished to remember, such as how I skillfully guided my new husband to keep him from stepping on my dress during our first dance, he also caught events that I otherwise would not have even known about. For example, my husband and I loved the fact that the video showed us what happened at the cocktail hour while we enjoyed the "seclusion" portion of the evening that occurs after the ceremony and before the reception. And, indeed, during much of the wedding, we were so focused on us that it's only afterwards that we were able to appreciate the broader perspective that the video provided. (For instance, who knew that Aunt Zelda could dance?) We also appreciated the flow of the video: Rather than just seeing stills of a dance, for example, the video showed us movements, such as how my husband and I started swaying together to the sounds of Andrew's serenade.

Given that I think a videographer enhances the wedding experience, I want to show you how to negotiate so that you can hire one and marvel at your video but not pay too much for it. To start, here are some basics about the process of hiring a videographer. As usual, you should calculate your bottom line to figure out what is the maximum you are willing to spend. Then take somebody impartial and objective with you to visit various videographers (or photographers who offer videography services) and ask them to let you view an entire video rather than just a short demo tape. This is important because a demo may have been specially enhanced and so it may not be representative of the videographer's typical work. You don't necessarily have to watch the whole video (we all know that brides-to-be have no free time), but feel free to ask the videographer to skip around the video and get a sense of the complete work. Notice the quality of the camera work and whether everything you'd like to have filmed is actually covered.

You want good quality, but of course you also want a good price. So investigate the range of prices and services offered by various studios. And don't forget to ask about potential discounts. You might try the direct approach, asking simply,

"What discounts or specials are you offering now?"

Or you could include some reason why you should be entitled to a discount. For example:

"Given that I was referred to you by another client and would like to return the favor, can you give me a break on the video?"

In fact, an interesting psychology study found that citing a reason—any reason—can increase the chances that someone will agree to your request. In the study, individuals making copies were approached by someone who asked to "cut in" and use the copier before they had finished with it. When the person provided a reason ("Can I use the copier? I'm in a hurry."), individuals were more likely to agree to the request than when no reason was provided. Amazingly, this result held even when the reason given was completely redundant with the request ("Can I use the copier? I need to make copies."). So saying anything, even if it conveys no new information (why else would someone need to use the copier?) can increase the likelihood that another party will accede to a demand.

Other reasons you can give are that you'd like to go with the videographer recommended by the photographer if the price is right, or you can mention that you are "considering other videographers at this point in time"—this veiled threat may prompt the studios to quote you a discounted price.

In addition to collecting information by meeting with various videographers, it's always a good idea to talk to others, such as family and friends or past clients, who have actually seen the person's work. Experts warn that soliciting someone from a list of recommended videographers provided by a reception hall may be risky, as sometimes the halls receive payments in return for placing certain individuals on their list of preferred service providers. According to one source, you can even get referrals from a local Videographer's Association. (Who knew there were such things?) Regardless, as I mentioned, I recommend always viewing a videographer's work before making a selection.

Should I Order the Videography/Photography Combo?

Negotiating for a videographer is generally made a little easier by the fact that you can often hire a videographer from the same company as the photographer's. In other words, when you meet with your photographer, you can generally also discuss hiring a videographer. The advantage of this joint negotiation is that a photographer and videographer from the same studio tend to work well together. Having worked together in the past means that they are often well coordinated; for example, they may be unlikely to intrude on each other's spaces, and they may even communicate better and give each other access to more information about you and your spouse than two strangers could.

For my wedding, after consulting with my photographer, the videographer knew to take the music from my first dance (Stevie Wonder's "You Are the Sunshine of My Life," in case you were curious) and set the closing of the wedding video to the same song. And when a technical problem at the site prevented him from filming my dance with my father, he was able to easily insert stills of the dance, again set to the appropriate music.

Granted there are occasionally disadvantages to hiring a videographer and a photographer from the same studio. Some experts warn of a lack of expertise on the part of a videographer who is primarily an adjunct to a photography studio, or they worry that hiring two people from the same studio increases the chances that both might miss your event. Some even cite a lack of divergent visual styles. However, I generally recommend hiring both from the same studio because of the tremendous advantage in terms of efficiency and ease for you, the sometimes-weary shopper.

Whether you choose to negotiate with a photographer and videographer together or with your videographer separately, once you've decided on which videography service you want, you should now prepare for a discussion to sign up that particular vendor. Luckily, many of the lessons we discussed regarding photographers apply here too! These include checking on the following:

- How long your videographer will be recording on your wedding day? Decide what start time and end time you'd like for the day, and make sure to allow the videographer time to set up and check equipment.
- How many hours of raw unedited tape footage will be recorded?
- What kind of turn around time there will be for you to receive the finished product (this can range

from "in-camera-edited," in which the video is presented to you at the end of your reception, all the way up to a year later)? The average is a few months.

C   How much ransom money you'll have to pay to keep the video from showing up on the internet? Okay, I'm kidding, but some experts do recommend reading the contact carefully to see whether the studio insists on retaining the copyright to the footage they've shot.

What to Negotiate

The Format: Video or DVD?

In thinking about what you want from a videographer, consider what happened to my friend Sherry. When she signed up for a videographer, she managed to negotiate for four copies of the wedding video—a pretty good deal, or so she thought. But she was more negotiation-minded than technology savvy. She got married at a point when digitial video discs or DVDs were becoming more popular (apparently, they were originally called digital versatile discs—who knew?). But she didn't realize that the trend was such that VCRs might soon become obsolete, and her photographer, negotiating on behalf of the videographer, certainly didn't enlighten her to this fact.

At the very least, the photographer could have mentioned that DVDs have a much longer shelf-life than videotapes—and that's assuming you're not playing them practically every day, like I do with my wedding video (okay, I admit it: I'm a bit obsessed). Instead, he signed her up for a deal in which she received four videotaped versions of her wedding but no DVDs. In retrospect, it seems like he was trying to distract her with sweetness by agreeing to give her so many videotape copies while all the while hoping that she wouldn't notice that she was missing the key DVD version. Months later, when she requested a DVD, she found out it would cost extra. So the lesson here is that if you'd like to preserve your video for posterity, make sure to specify in the contract that you receive a DVD in addition to (or in place of) a videotape.

What's in the Video?

At a minimum, a videographer tapes the ceremony and the reception. For many couples this coverage of the wedding day suffices. But let's say that you would like the video to include a montage of snapshots of you and your groom growing up. Or you want to add text or other special effects. Or let's say that you'd like to have a record of other aspects of your wedding, such as the rehearsal dinner or even of the honeymoon. (The latter is best accomplished by adding in footage that you provide—most folks don't invite the videographer along with them on their honeymoon!) You may have erroneously assumed that some of this would be covered when you hired the videographer. Or you may have forgotten to ask about these add-ons, but later learn that they are not covered, or maybe you realized that you might have to pay to add extras later, but at the time of signing, you weren't sure what you wanted. The thing is, these features almost always do cost extra, so much so that adding them may dramatically affect the price of the video.

Therefore it's a good idea to ascertain in advance what features come with the video for the quoted price. If there are extras included that you don't desire, ask to have them removed and have the price reduced. If there are extras included that you do desire, make sure that they are included in the contract so that the videographer won't attempt to double bill you for them later on. If no extras are included, but you'd like them to be, tell the videographers what package you want and solicit bids for the most inclusive offer at the lowest price, a la comparison shopping, as I mentioned above with wedding photography. At the very least asking about extra features ensures that you won't be surprised later on.

Editing the Tape

Once the raw footage has been recorded, normally the videographer begins editing the tape. But hold on a moment! Not so fast. Maybe you want to look at the footage first to see what essentials must be kept and what embarrassing moments should never be included in the video. Sounds like a good idea to me, but is the videographer going to charge you extra for the privilege of previewing the tape? It's best to be clear on this point beforehand. Maybe you can watch for free, in which case you should make sure that option appears in the contract. Perhaps there's a cost, which you can ask to be removed. The best way to accomplish this could be by adding your own nibble, in which you tell the videographer something like,

"I'm ready to sign with you; I just want to make sure I can view the tape before you edit it."

Given that extra work is not required in order to let you look at the video (if anything, you're helping with the editing process), you should not have to pay for this privilege.

Consider also what happens if the videographer omits something essential from the tape. Will there be an additional charge to try to correct the oversight? This was almost the case with me. My videographer did a wonderful job overall, but he left out something crucial: the precious father-daughter dance! It turns out he had failed to shoot this footage, but after some negotiating (and a lot of persistence on my part), he agreed to insert still photographs of me dancing with my dad at no additional cost. In the end, I was quite pleased with the result, but I certainly would not have been if I had had to pay extra to correct his mistake!

In terms of the finished product, I recommend that the video be less than two hours. Think of your wedding video like a feature film: Unless it's on a par with *Titanic*, most people aren't going to want to watch something that's substantially longer than a typical movie (and if it is on a par with *Titanic*, you should make sure your wedding has a better ending).

Other Details

One can get rather obsessive about every aspect of videography. For example, how many cameras will be used? Will any be digital? Will they all be manned or will some be remotely controlled from a central location? Will there be live editing or will that be done later? What kind of lighting will be needed? While some of these may be important to you, the one I believe is most important to worry about is the sound quality of the video.

Just recently, I attended a wedding at a beautiful horticultural center. The officiate was a New-Age minister who talked and sang for more than two hours. Which, even given the uncomfortable chairs, wouldn't have been so bad, except that none of the guests could hear a word she said (or sang). This might not have been so bad if the videographer had equipped her with a microphone so at least her words would be recorded for posterity. But he didn't, and the video camera, stationed among the guests, didn't pick up anything either. You should make sure the videographer uses the right type of microphone for your setting, so that every "I will" and "I do" gets recorded (especially when your spouses says the "love, honor, and obey" part). If your videographer uses wireless microphones or even the newer technology of remote digital recorders, just don't do what one of my male friends did and forget to take off the microphone when using the bathroom (and you thought that only happened in the *Naked Gun* movies).

Contract Fundamentals

In summary, then, here is what experts recommend should be included in a standard videography contract:

- The name and contract information of the videographer.

- The date; location(s) (with addresses) for the ceremony and reception (and additional places you'd like to be filmed, such as getting ready at home); starting time; number of hours.

- Number of assistants aiding the videographer as well as the type of equipment used.

- Length of video/DVD and number of these issued to you.

- Responsibilities for materials if video is lost or damaged.

- Date that the completed video will be finished (and, possibly, date the unedited video will be ready for you to view).

- Cost of video (and other charges, such as additional features or extra copies).

- Deposit amount due.

- Balance due date.

- Cancellation and refund policy.

- Any special instructions, such as key moments or people you wish to capture.

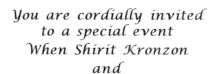

You are cordially invited
to a special event
When Shirit Kronzon
and
Andrew Ward
Join together in this chapter
To help you negotiate
the purchase of
wedding invitations.

Savings and success to follow.

Chapter Nine

Invitations

I nvitations are like a movie trailer for your wedding. These days nearly every movie in a theater is preceded by one or more previews of upcoming attractions. Indeed, sometimes there are so many, it's hard to keep track of which preview goes with which movie. But if it's a really good preview, chances are you'll remember the movie and be all the more excited to see it when it actually comes out. Well, think of your wedding invitations the same way; part of their purpose is to get your guests excited for your upcoming nuptials. Just like a movie with a lot of pre-release buzz, your special day can be something that guests eagerly anticipate and willingly shell out lots of bucks (or at least bring an expensive gift) to attend.

Some people don't give invitations a lot of thought, their reasoning being that the invites merely convey key logistical information about the day, such as the date, time, and location of the blessed event. But invitations give guests a first impression of your wedding, a preview of what it might look like. Will your wedding be very religious and formal? Or perhaps romantic with lots of flowers? Maybe yours will be a theme wedding like that of singer Toni Braxton, who incorporated a Tiffany's theme throughout her festivities, including a cake that looked like one of those famous blue boxes. I'm assuming there was no actual jewelry in the cake (could be a choking hazard)!

Whatever the style of your wedding, a good invitation, like a memorable movie preview, stands out amid the junk mail and portends a special event. Of course, the style of that invitation should ideally match the wedding itself. For example, a fun fanciful invite with an outline of Mickey Mouse's ears (yes, that option is available) should not accompany a formal wedding held in a museum. I mean, I suppose it would if you're planning to get married at Disney World. Likewise, a royalty-themed linen-finish deckle-edged invitation featuring a castle motif does not typically go with a wedding on a beach. For my own wedding (in case you're curious), I wanted to convey my Israeli heritage so I chose an invitation that showed an artistic rendering of a Temple in Jerusalem and included writing in Hebrew as well as in English. Even though my non-Israeli guests couldn't understand the Hebrew (including my very own husband), the guests knew to look forward to some Israeli traditions that were strongly incorporated in my wedding (Andrew claims his back is still sore from all that lifting during the chair dance).

Now, I'm not saying all this to put more pressure on you. The style of invitation is by no means the most critical choice you have to make regarding your wedding. I wouldn't, for example, recommend picking a future spouse based on how his last name will look in calligraphy. I'm only suggesting that you might not want to treat the wedding invites as merely an afterthought. And by all means, don't skimp on the envelope glue—it could be deadly! (Just kidding—if you're confused, ask a friend to tell you about that *Seinfeld* episode, the single most famous example of the hazards of shopping for wedding invitations.)

At the same time, there's no need to spend an exorbitant amount of money. Experts estimate that invitations should cost approximately five percent of your total wedding budget. That means the average couple will spend around $600 for invitations to a wedding with 175 guests. That comes out to over $3 per invitation, plus postage. Speaking of postage, if you order invitations approximately four months before your wedding, you should receive them at least two months prior to the event. That gives you sufficient time to mail them out about six to eight weeks before the wedding, meaning you should be in good shape to receive RSVPs several weeks in advance of your special day.

Before you start bargain shopping for invites, I advise you to collect all the relevant content information, such as names of the hosts (including how they will be titled on your invitation), the location of your ceremony and reception along with the date and time of the respective events, the address to which RSVPs should be sent, and the menu options, if guests are going to be required to make a food choice ahead of time. One final piece of advice before we get down to bargaining secrets and strategies: When it comes to the content, you can't proofread enough. In fact, I recommend that you enlist a friend to go over everything after you have. Ask him or her to double-check that you've spelled all names correctly and included accurate directions and, if necessary, a map (one way in which the internet has improved our lives is that companies such as MapQuest (*www.MapQuest.com*) allow you to download driving directions, however sometimes they're not *entirely* accurate). You might also get a sense of how much everything weighs for proper postage purposes.

Entrapment

The standard wedding invitation, like the standard wedding cake, is multi-layered. There's the outer envelope (which will be stamped and addressed); an unsealed inner envelope (which contains the actual contents and serves as extra protection in case the outer envelope gets damaged in the mail); the invitation itself, a reception card if the reception will be held at a different location than the ceremony; a response card featuring its own self-addressed, stamped envelope; and assorted other items such as printed directions, hotel information, pieces of tissue paper, and so on.

As you may have already discerned, this piecemeal approach to invitation construction lends itself to lots of ways to charge you more money. Even beyond these "basics" of the invite, you may find yourself (with the salesperson's help) considering more and pricier options for your invitations. This, naturally, represents a prime opportunity for entrapment: The longer you meet with the vendor, the more resources (that is, money) you may find yourself committing in order to fashion the most elaborate spectacle of an invitation this side of Buckingham Palace.

Of course it doesn't help that often terms are being bandied about that are, shall we say, not always the most familiar. I, for one, had no idea about things like vellum paper or blind-embossing. Yet these terms figured prominently in my discussions with vendors. Even choosing simpler elements, such as ink color, can quickly get out of hand. For instance, you may go into the process thinking that a standard black, gray, or even colored ink will be fine, but the salesperson may try to lead you toward nonstandard inks, that is, ones that include slight shades of silver or gold and happen to be much more costly. And let's not forget that the more ink colors you use, the pricier the proposition.

Similarly, the salesperson might encourage you to engrave your invitation, but I'm here to tell you that "you don't need an engraved invitation" to get married. (You knew that was coming!) You probably also don't need textured paper or what's called a deckle edge (an irregular "torn" edge characteristic of handmade paper) unless you're planning to prepare voting ballots for Florida. But these options, and others—envelopes emblazoned with a family crest, calligraphically designed scrolls for each place-setting, and so on—can be yours for the asking, or even if you don't ask! Speaking of calligraphy, you can also do calligraphy for each address for anywhere from $2.50 to $7 per envelope. For an entire invitation (inner and outer envelopes, plus return address on response cards), it can cost around $15 per head, so if you are planning on a large wedding, you might go with just the envelope. And don't make the mistake that one of Andrew's friends made: They addressed each envelope with calligraphy that was so ornate—and so illegible—that some of the invitations couldn't be delivered by the post office!

How to Handle It

1. Beware of Framing Effects

When purchasing wedding invitations, you should be careful not to become entrapped by the particular frame used by the salesperson. Let me explain: The cost of invitations can be described as either a price for the whole batch or in terms of the price per invitation. Imagine, for example, that a standard invitation for 100 people costs $500 total. You can focus your understanding of this price as either only $5 per invite or, of course, $500 total. If the invitations are framed individually, the $5 price may not seem too steep. After all, a greeting card at your nearest drugstore might cost nearly as much. When you are then encouraged to add embellishments such as special jacquard paper or a variegated ribbon, which raise the price from $5 to, say, $7.50, it's easy to justify spending only

$2.50 more. On the other hand, if you think in the aggregate, an additional $2.50 an invite of course amounts to a more hefty-seeming $250 overall.

In short, in order to guard against such effects, don't let someone else frame the price for you; choose the frame that best protects you and your money. For example, you might first go to several stationery stores to get a feel for what you like in the way of invitations. Then, when discussing these options with salespersons, don't let them lead you astray by quoting only a per-invite price. You might remind yourself of this pointer by always asking for the cumulative price for the entire service:

"Can you explain the price to me in terms of the total cost?"

If the salesperson resists, I encourage you to engage in calculations out loud that convert individual prices to totals:

"So, if each invite is approximately $8,
then 125 invites will cost me $1200."

Repeat this conversion process aloud as many times as is needed, even if it makes the salesperson think you are imitating Dustin Hoffman's character from *Rain Man*. It will help you maintain a more realistic perspective that will, in turn, help you resist unnecessary spending.

2. Hold to Your Bottom Line

Another way to discourage spending too much is to simply write down ahead of time the total amount you are willing to spend on invitations. That way, even if a vendor tries to entrap you with extra frills (do you really need marble-finish paper and mylar-lined envelopes?) you can handle it by simply saying something such as:

"If you could add that in, free of charge, I'd be grateful.
Otherwise, [insert amount] is all that I can afford."

Bringing somebody objective with you may help as well by
backing you up when the salesperson tries to persuade you to
spend more than you would like. In addition, when it's time to
leave a deposit, bring a check for a predetermined amount in
advance, which is typically half the total charge (on average
$300). If the check is already written and it's the only one you
brought, it will be all the more difficult to write a new one for
a larger amount.

Bait and Switch

Once you know what you'd like for your invitation, it's
important to ensure that that's what you actually get. For my
wedding, choosing an invitation style took several visits to the
relevant vendor—visits that included poring over sample books,
looking at paper design and quality, and choosing the lettering
style, ink color, and printing method, not to mention compos-
ing the precise wording of the invitation. Finally my fiancé
and I settled on something we liked and received an estimate
from the store of $800 for the complete service.

We decided to sleep on it—something, by the way, I advise you to do when dealing with all of your vendors. Postpon-
ing the closing of the deal, even if only for a day, shifts the
power balance toward you. The vendor is left wondering why
you didn't complete the order on the spot. Will you come
back? And will he or she have to give you a discount to seal
the deal if you return? For your part, although you may be
sorely tempted to close the deal during your first visit to a
particular vendor, I think that returning for a second meeting generally makes sense. It may, for example, encourage
the vendor to throw in something extra. Or you could ask

for something additional, implying that if you receive it, you are ready to sign. At the very minimum, by not immediately jumping at a purchase, you demonstrate that you are a careful shopper who does not casually commit to spending large amounts of money.

However, if you employ this strategy of delay, a word of warning. When a bride I know decided to sleep on an offer and returned to the invitations store a few days later, the sales representative announced that a special symbol she had wanted on the front of the invitation would cost $300 extra. Yikes! What to do? Let's think this through together. Here she is, ready to close the deal, when the sales agent changes the terms of that deal, making it less attractive to the customer. This tactic is known as *bait and switch*, and we've seen it used elsewhere. A salesperson gets a customer to agree to the basic terms of the deal, then changes the conditions, making them less favorable. In this particular instance, the tactic exploits the fact that by now, having spent many hours at the store, the bride had already become committed to the symbol she wanted and would therefore willingly shell out more money to obtain it.

How to Handle It

1. Get It in Writing

Had the bride gotten a written quote from the vendor during her first meeting, the salesperson's announcement would not have caused such a problem. She could have calmly produced the piece of paper and inquired about the inconsistency. Without it, she was left with the option of referring to a verbal agreement that the salesperson might not even remember making. Thus, whenever you ask for a price from a vendor, get that quote in writing. You can directly ask, "Could I get that quote in writing?" Or you can be a little subtler:

"Planning this wedding involves keeping track of so many things. If I don't have everything written down, I might forget what I was even doing at this store! Would you mind writing down the price you just quoted?"

If an establishment refuses to give you a quote, you might consider going elsewhere.

2. Just Say No

Even if you are initially thwarted by a vendor, don't give up. As with so much in life, persistence is the key. If a salesperson tries to add on an extra charge, refuse it, and calmly maintain that you expect to pay no more than the original quoted price (even if that quote wasn't written down). If need be, talk to a supervisor, perhaps saying the following:

"The last time I was in here, I received a quote of $X. Now that price has been raised. I would like to purchase invitations here, but, in turn, I would like for you to hold to the original quoted price."

That way, you make it clear that each of you is in some ways making a "concession": The vendor lowers the price and, in return, makes a sale to a (now) satisfied customer. Is this technique guaranteed to succeed? Why, yes. Yes, it is. Okay, it's not guaranteed, but if you don't ask, you guarantee yourself something else: Paying a higher price or not getting the item at all. As a wise person once said, if you don't ask, you don't give the other side the opportunity to say yes.

3. Insist on a Reciprocal Concession

Let's say that vendor refuses to lower the price. If that's the case, you can try to engender some reciprocity:

"Because you're asking me to pay a price that is higher than I was originally quoted, I would appreciate it if you could shave off a bit for X" (where X might be, say, the cost of some other extra such as fancy engraving or deluxe envelopes, like the ones that George Costanza should have purchased in that classic Seinfeld episode).

I have found that using the word "appreciate" can get you places. People like to be acknowledged, and remember that old quote attributed to various sources: "The key to life is sincerity. If you can fake that, you've got it made!" You can also make use of "if-then" statements, such as

"If I agree to pay $300, then I would hope to receive some extra invitations in case I make a mistake while addressing them and need to redo some."

4. Remember Your Alternatives

If nothing succeeds, there is, of course, always the threat of taking your business elsewhere. Our befuddled bride, for example, could tactfully bring up the fact that the wedding symbol in question could be purchased from another vendor.

"That additional charge you mentioned seems a bit puzzling, given that I've received another quote for the same symbol for considerably less somewhere else."

Notice that you're not saying: "You wanna charge me more? Fine! I'll take up my business elsewhere!" See the difference? While both versions employ a threat, the latter version invokes an explicit threat that may antagonize the other party and put them on the defensive. The salesperson may even call your bluff and invite you to take your invitation business elsewhere. On the other hand, an implicit threat allows the salesperson to save face and potentially return to the original price or even come up with a new discount. So make your implicit threat and see how the salesperson responds.

Surprise Fees

Let's say that you've compiled the various features that will comprise your invitation. With your chosen invitation in mind, you order the number of invitations you estimate you will need, plus a few more, just to be on the safe side. But what if somewhat later, your future in-laws make it known that they want to invite more guests? On the other hand, what if after you've sent your invitations, you discover that more people have declined than you had anticipated? You were counting on having a large number of people at your wedding. Not to mention the fact that you've already made catering arrangements based on the original number of invites. Now you're left scrambling to come up with an expanded guest list. Or maybe you've got the right number of invitations but you've discovered some smudging of addresses occurred in the mail, and a good number have been returned undelivered.

Imagine further that when you go back to order a few more invitations, you are shocked at the price. In fact, some invitations stores tack on a flat fee for this additional order, no matter how small the number you are purchasing. So it's best to order at least one or two-dozen extra invitations at the outset. You can always keep some as souvenirs of your special day.

Another surprise fee can come up during the proofing stage, that is, when you are making sure that the invitations accurately depict what you ordered. Typically, once you've made your order you will get the opportunity to proof the product before the final version is printed. But it will cost you! That fee may be small ($25) but it could add up if multiple mistakes, requiring multiple proofings, occur. While many vendors claim the proofing charge is mandatory, you can still try to negotiate.

How to Handle It

1. Ask to Have the Fee Waived

Saying something as simple as, "Is there a way that you could waive the proofing fee?" can be effective. As previously mentioned, sometimes just asking will be enough. Sometimes adding a reason—any reason—can be even more effective. For instance,

*"I would like you to remove the fee
because I was not aware of it,"*

or

*"I was hoping you could waive the fee because
I was hoping that there would not be a fee for this service."*

Notice that no new information is being conveyed in the latter alternative (why else would you want the fee waived!) But just adding the placebo-like reason at the end can increase the effectiveness of the request.

Did You Know?

In Greece, it is a wedding tradition to write the names of all single female friends and relatives of the bride on the sole of her shoe. After the wedding, the shoe is examined, and those whose names have worn off are said to be the next in line for marriage.

No fair writing your younger sister's name in indelible ink.

2. Have a Contingent Contract

If asking for a fee waiver fails, you can try to invoke a contingency—something such as the following:

"I'll tell you what: I will pay the proofing fee if I made an error; otherwise I'd appreciate it if you would waive the fee."

That way, both sides have an incentive to get it right.

Here are some handy tips for proofreading the invitations, courtesy of Lei Lydle, founder and editor of *www.WeddingBasics.com*:

- You should check the style, color, and font type to make sure they are exactly what you ordered.
- Check the spelling of the names of both the people and places involved.
- Make sure the proper titles are included.
- Look for special words such as *honour* and *o'clock* and make sure they are spelled correctly.
- Double check the date and time and make sure the day, date, time, and year are all written out and spelled correctly.
- Check on the accuracy of the address on both the return flap and the response card envelope.
- Check for punctuation such as commas between the city and state, periods after abbreviations, and so on.
- Make sure the layout and spacing looks okay.

Deadlines

One final issue to be aware of is deadlines. Make sure the vendor you deal with has given you a firm date for when you can expect to pick up your invitations. When the order comes in, experts recommend that before you leave the store, you should proofread one last time and count the number of invitations to ensure that everything is as it should be. And, of course, don't make your final payment until everything is letter perfect. Oh, I almost forgot: I'm happy to send you my current address so you can be sure the invitation is accurate. (Well, it was worth a try!)

Did You Know?

Rice has been used as a symbol of fertility and as a wish for a "full pantry" in various parts of the world from ancient to modern times. In the past, rice was not the only thing thrown at the bride and groom as they left the wedding. Wheat, instead of rice, was thrown in France, figs and dates were thrown in Northern Africa, and a combination of coins, dried fruit, and candy was thrown in Italy. In some European countries eggs are thrown! Flower petals, confetti, bubbles, and balloons are often used today instead of rice.

When throwing, just remember the rule: "Is it bigger than a breadbox?"

Chapter Ten

Negotiating *With* Family

W hen planning your wedding, you are going to want to take into account, at the very least, the wishes of your fiancé, who of course knows that the proper response to all your requests is "yes, dear." But it's more than likely that you will also be called upon to accommodate the wishes of your family as well, especially if they are helping to finance your nuptials. And then there are—gulp—your future in-laws. It can be challenging enough to have your family involved in planning your wedding, but to involve individuals whom you (or your family) may have only recently met can be downright intimidating. After all, a lot is at stake. You want the perfect wedding, but you don't want to alienate people. It's a scary proposition, isn't it?

I hope I can reassure you by saying that this is a natural part of the process. Let me say that again: It's only natural to be frightened at the prospect of discussing wedding plans with your family and especially your in-laws. It's just not that easy to plan a wedding with a whole other family. Because, let's face it: It's often a challenge just to get along with virtual strangers, let alone to plan a momentous event as you're getting to know them. But, fear not. In this chapter I'm going to give you strategies to help you with everything from resolving conflicts and accommodating different budgetary preferences to just plain getting along with your in-laws and, for that matter, your family, too. But first, a word (or 146 words, to be exact) of caution.

Don't Burn Your Bridges

In all of the wheelin' and dealin' we've covered, the negotiations were always with wedding vendors—most of whom, if all goes well, you'll be contacting with only once for a wedding. Negotiating with family is different. Unless you plan to move to a distant continent immediately after your wedding, you are likely to experience many more interactions over the years. Hardball negotiation tactics that might work wonders in one-time encounters may simply not be appropriate with people you expect to see again and again, especially if you care about preserving your relationship with these people. Negotiating in a manner that fails to take into account the interests of others may succeed at first, but eventually it can only lead to conflict and failed relationships. So if you want to have the wedding of your dreams without destroying future relationships, pay heed.

Did You Know?

Until relatively recently, brides were considered the property of their father. Their futures and husbands were arranged without their consent. The marriage of an unattractive woman was often arranged with a prospective groom from another town without either of them having ever seen their prospective spouse. In more than one instance, when the groom saw his future wife, usually dressed in white, for the first time on the day of the wedding, he changed his mind and left the bride at the altar. To prevent this from happening, it became "bad luck" for the groom to see the bride on the day of the wedding prior to the ceremony.

Now you know where they got the idea for a veil.

Integrative Bargaining

Experts in conflict resolution often suggest thinking about a negotiation not as an adversarial give-and-take, but rather as an opportunity for joint problem solving, or what they term *integrative bargaining*. This may be especially true for parties in longstanding relationships. Accordingly, rather than regarding your parents or in-laws as evil foes who are trying to ruin your wedding, try to view them members of a team that are all working toward the same goal: Giving you the best wedding possible. So if a family member offers a suggestion for your wedding that makes your skin crawl (for example, "How about we let Cousin Lenny's garage band do the music!"), the goal is not to dismiss it. Instead, try to get more information. For example, you might want to begin by responding with, "That's an interesting suggestion." *Interesting* is one of those nicely ambiguous words that can be put to good diplomatic use, as it doesn't automatically convey positive or negative sentiment. You can then follow that response with some clarifying questions, such as, "How did you come up with it?" and "Why are you in favor of it?" In that way, instead of simply rejecting the idea, which could lead to resentment, resistance, and escalating arguments, you've acted as if you are interested in problem-solving, and can consistently reframe difficult conversations as constructive discussions about how to plan a festive celebration. Here are additional suggestions to help facilitate agreement between you and your rancorous relatives.

Interests Versus Positions

In their groundbreaking work, *Getting to Yes* (Penguin, 1991), Harvard negotiation specialists Roger Fisher and William Ury introduced a critical distinction—one that can help you bargain integratively rather than simply knock heads with family members. They stressed the importance of negotiating in a way that defends interests rather than positions. Positions typically involve a demand and can both make you seem intransigent and alienate the other side. Underlying positions are interests, the basic values or priorities that make you who you are. Interests, especially ones rooted in basic principles (for example, fairness, equality, and kindness), are often less controversial and indeed are often shared by the other side (who doesn't like fairness?). So, when it comes to negotiating with family members, instead of making demands ("I insist on holding my wedding at this site"), you can try stating your interests instead ("I'm interested in having an outdoor wedding"). Even if your family doesn't initially favor your choice of venues, in hearing you articulate your interest, they are likely to respect the fact that you want an outdoor wedding and may even come up with another outdoor location that serves your interest as well as theirs.

Let's give another example. Imagine a bride and her mother who are at loggerheads over the size of the guest list. The bride wants no more than 50 guests; the mother wants 250. They go back and forth arguing their position. ("It's my wedding!" "But your father and I are paying for it!") Finally, they decide to compromise and invite 150, but neither of them is particularly happy about it. Why? Because the solution didn't address their underlying interests—interests that, in all the battling back and forth, never got stated. Suppose that the bride had been able to state her interests: "I want a small wedding because I want to be able to share all the precious moments with people who are my closest to me." Imagine that her mother had similarly been able to state her interests: "I want to invite a lot of guests because I don't want anyone in our family or friends to feel snubbed."

Such an exchange could have led both parties to a solution that would have made them happier than simply "splitting the difference." For example, all 250 guests could be invited but the bride could have absolute say over who gets to sit close to the bridal party table at the reception and who gets foisted off into the anteroom. That way, the bride gets to look into the faces of those she considers most dear all night, while third cousin Edna doesn't feel slighted for not being invited, especially because she's conveniently seated near the bar. Alternatively, the official wedding could be a small affair, but the bride's parents could hold a larger gathering later on to allow all their friends and relatives to partake in the festivities (heck, it worked for Queen Elizabeth when her son Charles got married the second time). The point is that, without discovering underlying interests and instead responding simply to stated positions, parties in conflict risk missing opportunities to achieve agreements that satisfy everyone's needs.

Let's try one more example, this one involving the make-up of the bridal party. Let's say the groom's mother envisions a ceremony in which her other son serves as best man or her daughter serves as maid-of-honor. But as the bride, you already have your best friend or sister in mind for those coveted roles. Or maybe you'd rather forgo the whole wedding party idea entirely. Thinking in terms of positions can escalate into a fight: "I would like my daughter to be a maid of honor." "I'd really prefer to have X be my maid of honor instead." Back and forth. Here is where interests make a difference. With some gentle probing, for example, you may learn that your mother-in-law's real interest lies in having her family adequately represented during the ceremony. Maybe you can meet this interest by letting your in-laws play prominent roles in the wedding without their needing to be ushers or bridesmaids. For example, perhaps said persons would be willing to read a poem, make a toast, or light a candle. Sometimes, being asked to play any official role is sufficient to placate a disgruntled family member.

My point in all of these examples is that instead of defending your particular preferences ("I'm going to elope if you won't let me invite my college roommate to the wedding!"), you defend principles ("I would like a wedding that includes people who are dear to me and can help me share the joy of the occasion"). As you can see, while positions can be flashpoints for conflict, it can be much more difficult for the other side in a negotiation to reject a principle—when stated that way, who wouldn't want a wedding to include close friends?

Trading Across Issues

Earlier I suggested that planning your wedding is likely to involve multi-party negotiations, but it's also likely to involve multiple issues as well. Fortunately, that can work to your benefit. Having several issues on hand to negotiate means that you can rank order them in terms of their importance to you. And your parents and in-laws can do the same. What you typically find is that there will be several issues that you consider critical that others will not; and vice-versa. You can then trade across these issues. You care about the location, your mother cares about the guest list; you get the location you want, she gets the guest list she wants. The process is called logrolling, named after the early American custom of neighbors helping each other roll logs into a pile for burning. For instance, when I got married, my top priority was having an outdoor wedding; my in-laws' most important priority was the menu for the reception dinner. We log-rolled our respective interests so that I chose the outdoor setting of my dreams and my in-laws had a say in choosing the food.

Similarly, you can allocate different parts of the wedding planning to different parties, depending on whose interests you most want to satisfy. Of course, that means you have to identify those interests, and, as I suggested previously, first asking all the relevant parties to spell out their priorities ahead of time can go a long way toward addressing everyone's needs. Naturally, in planning a wedding, not every decision is going to please every person. But because your parents and in-laws will likely pay for some portion of the wedding, they should have some say. Ideally it would be about issues that matter to them but don't matter to you.

However, if you find yourself in a situation in which everyone's priorities are nearly identical but interests are not (for example, everyone wants a say in who gets invited but nobody agrees on who it is that's getting one of the precious invitations), don't panic. First, remember it's your wedding and you should be the ultimate arbiter when it comes to resolving disagreements between various parties. Second, you may find that you can involve disagreeing family members in other parts of the wedding planning process that you consider less critical, such as finding lodging for distant relatives or choosing decorations. Even if they also initially consider such issues to be low priority items, the mere act of asking them to take on these particular details may cause them to re-evaluate. At the very least, they may feel grateful just to have their opinions acknowledged and respected, no matter how seemingly trivial the domain in question. So, for instance, if you really care about where the wedding will be held, rather than asking others to help pick a reception hall, they can decide how best to arrange the seating. Or, to take another example, rather than choosing the flowers, they can pick the type of container that will hold the flowers (for example, round or square, clear or opaque).

Acknowledge Your Concessions

Sometimes it's important not just to trade across issues but to ensure that the other side in a negotiation is aware that you are making a sacrifice. Otherwise the other side may persist in pushing you for even more concessions. Now, there's no need to go overboard here, but saying something like, "I realize that this issue is very important to you, and I want you to enjoy the day, so let's go with your option" can be both a kind gesture and a useful strategy. For example, if there is another issue for which you don't want to compromise, then a gentle reminder that you have already conceded on a previous issue can enhance your bargaining position.

Don't Over-Win

Negotiation experts use the term over-winning to describe a situation in which you have already exacted significant concessions from the other side but decide to press for more (for example, professional athletes who, unsatisfied with multimillion dollar contracts, decide to sit out the season unless all their demands are met—important demands, mind you, such as a full-time masseuse or someone to carry their bags at the airport). Nobody likes a poor winner—least of all the other side, so if you want to preserve your relationships with your family members, show some generosity. Indeed, you might initially demand more than you expect to get ("I want a five-course sit-down dinner!") and then concede some points, making it clear that you're doing so to please the other side. ("Okay, you win: four courses is fine.") Psychology studies show that such concessionary gestures can be effective in engendering good will.

Trading across issues is the most common way to resolve conflict. But here are four other tactics that just might come in handy as well:

Expand the Pie

So many conflicts have at their root the same problem: Scarce resources. There's only so much money, time, or good will to go around, right? Well, sometimes there's more than you think. People who engage in conflict resolution for a living know that sometimes the solution to a problem is to simply add new resources. For example, let's say you really want a DJ at your reception so you can have the latest hip music, but other members of your family—perhaps those who are a bit more senior—prefer a band that will play the classics. You don't necessarily have to go for one and not the other. You could have both: a band for the cocktail and dinner hours, and a DJ for the dancing portion. Will it cost more? Of course. Will it preserve harmony in the family and allow everyone to enjoy themselves. Almost certainly.

Or let's say there are only a limited number of spots in the bridal party and too many family members want in (yes, believe it or not, some people actually enjoying wearing a bridesmaid's dress). The solution? As I mentioned earlier, come up with more slots—greeters, readers, people to pass out programs, the official napkin folder—be creative!

Buy Them Off

Sometimes the best way to ensure you get what you want in a negotiation is literally to pay off the other side—folks in the biz call it nonspecific compensation. Okay, handing your mother-in-law a wad of cash is probably not going to keep her from complaining about your choice of caterer. But pointing out to her that, by going with a less expensive food service provider, you now have enough money left over to take her to her favorite spa the week before the wedding might be an effective alternative. Nonspecific compensation is similar to logrolling. But here is the difference: With logrolling, there are already issues on the table that you exchange. With nonspecific compensation, new incentives or resources are introduced that you then exchange. So in a way, nonspecific compensation is a combination of enlarging the pie and logrolling.

Make It Easy for Them to Say Yes

Often parties to a dispute don't want to concede anything because they imagine worst-case scenarios. Help them to realize that by saying yes, they're really not giving up as much as they think they are. In other words, minimize the costs associated with them saying yes. As an example, as I mention in Chapter 3, when I got married, my in-laws were worried that an outdoor ceremony would be unbearable (not an unreasonable concern, given that it was August in Philadelphia and, unlike me, most of the guests did not grow up in the desert). To make matters more manageable, we agreed to hold a relatively short ceremony outdoors, allowing everyone to wait in air-conditioned comfort until the banquet manager gave the signal that the wedding would commence immediately. Everyone's pain was minimized—well everyone except Andrew, but then I told him not to wear that wool suit! ("But, Shirit, it looked so good!")

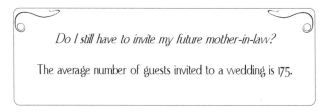

Do I still have to invite my future mother-in-law?

The average number of guests invited to a wedding is 175.

Please Everyone

You've heard time and time again that you can't please everyone. And that's true, but many times with just a little creative thinking, a solution can be arrived at that meets most of the needs of everyone involved in a dispute. For example, if you and your family can't agree on what music to play at your wedding, find a DJ who will play an eclectic mix—something contemporary for you and something classical for your family.

I particularly recommend this tactic for interfaith weddings, which often must be handled with extra delicacy. Rather than fight over whose cultural heritage will be neglected, the bride and groom can create a new culture that incorporates their favorite elements from both of their respective traditions. For example, you can have a priest and rabbi share the ceremony duties. You can include the breaking of the glass from the Jewish tradition, and hymns from the Catholic tradition. Prayers and readings can be drawn from both traditions.

Time to take stock. We've reviewed a number of different strategies and tactics to facilitate agreement between you and various family members. Although some are more nuanced than others, all have at their core the same two principles: Try to understand the other side's perspective and don't be bound into rigid categories. With a little sensitivity and creativity, you can have the wedding you always wanted and not lose family members in the process. After all, a wedding is one day; a family is forever.

The Money Issue

Thus far we have dealt with how to reconcile differences in taste or preference when it comes to various wedding options; for example, you want to get married in June but your mother prefers September. You want a band, your in-laws favor a DJ. These are important, of course. But in some ways we've been skirting around a more fundamental problem, and that, of course, is the thorny issue of money. Perhaps your mother prefers September because it is off-season and rates will be cheaper. Or your in-laws prefer a DJ over a band because they have someone in mind who will be inexpensive. Maybe you want an expensive dress but your father keeps insisting that "you'll only wear it once." I've given you strategies to help you get that fancy dress for less when negotiating with the vendor. But how do you convince your own parents that it's worth the money you (or maybe even they) are spending? In this section I want to help you better communicate with your family and in-laws about the touchy subject of wedding finances.

As I've already suggested, if either set of parents is helping to pay for the wedding, then you'll have to include them in the decision making on some level. It's my belief that they should have a say over matters that involve them. For instance, they might have strong opinions about the type of accommodations offered to guests or the number of invitations issued. It is their family after all. So here is where you might want to be flexible, in that they should be entitled to include their family, friends, and business associates as potential guests. Likewise you are also entitled to your family, friends, and business associates. And if that means the list becomes excessively long, then show it to both sets of parents—maybe then they'll be motivated to make some cuts. And, when it comes to people they've invited, let them make the cuts; no need for you to decide who among their friends is worthy to attend. If you have to, feel free to invoke a principle (for example, "We're looking at an all-adult wedding" or "We're intending to favor family over work acquaintances"), but let them worry about instantiating that principle.

Of course, other wedding issues that are more centrally about you, like the style of your dress or the kind of music you prefer for your first dance, should normally be decided by you, even if someone else is paying. For instance, let's say you want your first dance to be a rumba/salsa combination because you recently took a dance class and, having caught the Latin fever, you want to try those sexy new moves. But let's say that your parents keep hinting, in a not-so-subtle way, that they look forward to seeing you waltz because they prefer a traditional dance. Well, here's a domain in which your preference should dominate because only you and your groom will be dancing. You might nod and say "Thanks for your viewpoint; we'll take it into account" and then do what you want. If need be, you can tell them that while you will be doing the salsa, it's not like you'll be doing the Lambada—anybody remember that one? Of course, it pays to be reasonable: You could, for example, ensure that when the parents are called to the floor to dance, their style of music is played. And just because you want to try your sexy new dance moves, there's no reason to go overboard; save something for the hotel room that night!

In general, when dealing with disagreements with family members, I recommend that the bride and groom each be responsible for dealing with his or her own parents. The bride should communicate with her parents and the groom should handle his. As an engaged friend was once told by a priest, "Your family, your problem." You don't want to put the groom in the awkward position of arguing with his in-laws, and that's not a good way for you to forge a new relationship with yours (after all, at some point down the road, you're gonna want a babysitter). Regardless of how you handle matters between yourself and your intended, the two of you should present a united front when facing parents or other family members—what folks in the negotiation business call being monolithic (literally, "one stone"). So be clear with each other how you want to handle various challenges presented by others, and then stick to your (unified) plan. Negotiation experts know that getting your own side to reach consensus can be even more difficult than reaching agreement with the other side, so it's best to tackle any disagreements with your future spouse first, then worry about achieving unanimity with parents or in-laws.

Of course, in all your dealings with family members, it's important to act on actual information, not assumptions. For example, I have a friend who simply assumed his parents would pay for half of his wedding. He conveyed this information to his bride-to-be, who in turn told her parents. Things got a little awkward when it turned out the information was, shall we say, less than accurate. Some sources recommend formulating a list of all the elements of a wedding that will require financial backing and circulating it among family and in-laws, just so there are no misunderstandings.

Remember that just as being rude or hostile can lead to failed agreements and protracted conflict, so can a failure to share relevant information. So don't be afraid to have honest conversations with family members. Sometimes asking a direct question can be called for: "What do you imagine spending on this wedding?" Other times being indirect may be the best strategy: "Susie's parents are contributing $10,000 toward her wedding. What do you think of that?" Note that in the past, the bride's family could be expected to foot the majority of the bill for the wedding. These days, there are no hard and fast rules for who should pay for what, so it behooves you to come to some sort of agreement with all interested parties as to how the costs will be split. You might make use of fair-seeming allocations, such as a 50/50 split between the two families; or 1/3 from your family, 1/3 from your in-laws, and 1/3 from you and your groom; or maybe one side will pay for the rehearsal dinner and costs associated with the ceremony itself, whereas the other side pays for the reception.

Just remember that, in any discussion with family members, whether it be about money or any other aspect of the wedding, encourage everyone to share their underlying interests, not their superficial positions. Listen carefully and restate their position if necessary ("What I hear you saying..."), and don't immediately dismiss any idea, no matter how ludicrous. There'll be plenty of time down the road to conveniently "forget" your father-in-law's suggestion that you should hold your reception at his favorite pub. Finally, if something rubs you the wrong way, there's no need to attack, just focus on your feelings ("I feel a little hurt by that suggestion"). Inevitably, there will be disagreements; how you handle those disagreements will not just determine whether your wedding goes smoothly, but it will help set the tone for your future relationship with your family—and his.

Now go have the wedding—and the marriage—of your dreams!

Bibliography

Books

Linda Babcock and Sara Laschever. *Women Don't Ask: Negotiation and the Gender Divide.* Princeton, NJ: Princeton University Press, 2003.

Herb Cohen. *You Can Negotiate Anything.* New York: Bantam Books, 1982

Roger Fisher and William Ury. *Getting to Yes, 2nd edition.* NewYork: Penguin Publishing, 1991.

G. Richard Shell. *Bargaining for Advantage.* New York: Penguin Publishing, 1999.

Douglas B. Smith. *Ever Wonder Why?* New York: Ballantine Books, 1991.

Websites

The Bridal Association of America
  BridalAssociationofAmerica.com

ButlerWebs.com
  butlerwebs.com

Elegant Bride magazine
  ElegantBride.com

Maryland's Eastern Shore Wedding Guide
MDBrides.com

SmartMoney.com
SmartMoney.com

The Knot
TheKnot.com

Top Wedding Links
TopWeddingLinks.com

UltimateWedding.com
UltimateWedding.com

WeddingBasics.com
WeddingBasics.com

WeddingeXpress
WeddingExpress.com

7BlueSeas
7BlueSeas.com

Index

About *the* Authors

Shirit Kronzon received her bachelor's degree in psychology from Stanford University and her Ph.D. in social psychology from Princeton University. She has been a member of the faculty of the Wharton School of Business of the University of Pennsylvania for more than seven years, where she has taught a variety of applied psychology courses, including negotiation, leadership, and organizational behavior, to business executives, Management of Business Administration (MBA) students, and undergraduates. She has published research in the fields of negotiation and decision-making.

Andrew Ward is a faculty member of the Psychology Department of Swarthmore College. He received his B.A. in biology from Harvard University and his Ph.D. in psychology from Stanford University. His research interests include conflict and negotiation, and the self-regulation of emotions, behaviors, and thoughts. He has published a number of scholarly journal articles and book chapters, and his work has been featured in such popular magazines as *Glamour, Self, Allure,* and *Redbook.*